Writing the Diaphragm Blues
And
Other Sexual Cacophonies

By

Rebecca Lea McCarthy

Copyright

Writing the Diaphragm Blues
And
Other Sexual Cacophonies

Find out more about the author online:

Website: http://Rebeccamccarthy.com
Twitter: @Rebaenrose
Facebook: https://www.facebook.com/DiaphragmBlues

Dedication

This work is dedicated to all people who have ever stood in front of a mirror naked, contemplating the lot of it.

Table of Contents

Foreword

A note about this book

This book presents scholarship and argument using a combination of memoir, traditional research, social media, creative writing, theatre/comedy and "standpoint theory." As argued by Donna Haraway in her 1988 article "Situated Knowledges: The Science Question in Feminism and the Privilege of Partial Perspective," for Feminist Studies: "Feminist objectivity is about limited location and situated knowledge, not about transcendence and splitting of subject and object" (583). Critics of standpoint theory, such as rhetorical scholar M. Lane Bruner, correctly warn of the pitfalls of reinforcing gender stereotypes though identity politics, since argumentation can easily become a narrow monologue, a singular rhetorical act (See: Bruner, M. Lane. "Producing Identities: Gender Problematization and Feminist Argumentation." *Argumentation & Advocacy* 32 [1996]: 185-98.). This work acknowledges that inspiration for scholarship and argument stem from the agency of the self and situated knowledge. However, as scholars, readers and people living everyday life, it is our responsibility to acknowledge our situated knowledge and identity politic standing, and then extend from the self to a wider audience and community.

Introduction
Writing the Diaphragm Blues

Why did the diaphragm cross the road?
It was afraid of a "head-on" collision. #birthcontrol #Joke

Have you ever noticed how strange and absurd the world of sexuality is? Maybe this strangeness is simply a result of all the social rites and moral "thou shall," and "thou shall nots" around sex and sexuality. Without a doubt, our culture makes a great deal of fuss about sex. Having sex. Having good sex. Having sex all the time. Not having sex all the time. Having sex to procreate. Having sex for the hell of it. Who one can have sex with. Who one should not have sex with. In what positions can one have sex, and so on and so forth. As a culture, we are preoccupied about our obsession with sex and sexuality. If general sexuality is strange, then female sexuality is strange times ten, its stranger because female sexuality is subjected to more rules, regulations, and moral framing than male sexuality. Of course this is also true for groups standing outside the "normal" realm of sexuality, including gays and lesbians, transgendered, transvestites, and anyone who is not practicing conventional "bacon and eggs" sexuality.

Nevertheless, I want to focus on gender. In general, the female gender has been highly regulated when it comes to sexuality. This is for many reasons: women can give birth, women are more likely to step into the role of family caregiver,

5

and women are seen as second-class citizens. This is as true today as it was fifty years ago, as it was one hundred years ago, as it was two hundred years ago, and even thousands of years ago. Just because something feels "traditional," does not mean it's right or "natural." After all, slavery was argued for within the framework of what was "natural" and "traditional" as well. Whether we like it or not, even in the United States of America, women are still considered second-class citizens. If this were not true, women would make the same amount of money for performing the same job as their male counterparts. Women's sexuality would not be regulated, and there would not be this ongoing struggle for women's right to birth control. If men gave birth, birth control would be a no brainier. But no. Women can't be trusted not to sleep with every Tom, Dick, or Harry if they are allowed birth control.

Why did the diaphragm cross the road?
All the Johns were there. #birthcontrol #joke

The "usual" solution? Treat women like objects, rather than independent, autonomous beings. Seen as a simple object, one can control and use a woman. Sadly, this "tradition" and so-called "natural" arrangement between the sexes can lead to serious violence. Consider the fact that in many countries, women become weapons of war when they are raped in order to destroy a community by harming its population and introducing "enemy" DNA.[1]

Honestly, shouldn't a woman be treated the same as her male counterpart in all things? She should be given the same respect, and guaranteed the same rights under the law. Yet even in 2012, the equal rights amendment has not passed, having only 35 out of the needed 38 states (a three-quarter majority) to ratify the ERA as the 28th Amendment to the

---

[1] Smith-Spark. "How did rape become a weapon of war?" *BBC News*. 12 August 2004. Web. 7 October 2012.

Constitution. Why? Women's sexuality? Yes I believe that is part of the answer. For some reason sex is equated with gender inequality: a so-called preordained, natural, and hierarchical arrangement of relations:

HIERARCHICAL GODS
(In a collective voice) Line up humans. All right, anything with a penis goes first!

ME
Does that count for vibrating ones, because I got a few of those! I got three! Goody, I get to be first!

HIERARCHICAL GODS
(Under their collective breath)

Christ.

(To the group of humans standing around) Never mind that. The new rule is this: anyone with boobs must go second!

ME
Hell, I've got nada up there! That means you, you with the man-bra over there, you be LAST! HA! You should have gotten off the couch more often.

MAN-BRA WEARING MAN
Give me a break, will you? The Angelical season just ended. Who could miss a series between the Angels and the Devils! We had some hot tailgating this year!

When defining "natural" as the way things have to be, the way they should be, then there is nothing "natural" about ranked gender arrangements. It is as natural as the man-bra and I know a lot of men who would protest to using a man-

7

bra, even if it would "naturally" put things back up where they "naturally" belong. These are simply social constructions created to keep things the way people feel they ought to be, not how they should be. Gender inequality is a social construction and an embedded one at that. This means society takes it for granted that when it comes to status, women are second to men. It is the same logic that leads me to choose chocolate over strawberry ice cream, or Charmin bathroom tissue over a different brand. Even if we don't think these words specifically (for example, men totally rock and women totally don't), our social actions and laws say differently. Surely, this is why the equal rights amendment has not passed (come on people, it was introduced in 1923 for Hierarchical God's sake), and it is also why during the 2012 election cycle women were challenged about whether or not they should be allowed to have easy access to birth control. Not only allowed to have easy access, but in some cases whether a woman should be allowed to use birth control at all. In the end, this social construction is a bad joke.

Why did the diaphragm walk across the road?
It didn't, rubber bounces, silly! #birthcontrol #joke

When I was young, it never occurred to me that I couldn't do anything I wanted to do in this world. My mom was quite adamant about this idea, encouraging me to seek whatever profession, lifestyle, and horizon I wanted to bring to my world and my life. My mom was what you might call a radical. She was very open and frank with her two daughters, and she fought for women's rights most of her life. In some ways, my mom's absolute belief in my rights as a woman allowed me to grow up taking these rights for granted to some degree, assuming that the rights of women were no different from the social or legal rights awarded men. Whether talking about careers, education, or sexual choices, there was a part of me that assumed the whole "life field" was equal between the sexes. I didn't have to grow up so very much to find out how very wrong this assumption was, or that the reason for this inequality could be found between my legs and on my chest. Generally, the social construction of genderism was built out of "my" physical body. The fact I could have babies, that this was part of my physical makeup, somehow made me different. The fact I had breasts somehow made me different. The fact I was missing a penis somehow made me different, and less. These differences made me not only separate, but also unequal. This was all learned very early in life, from my interactions with friends and with the larger world around me. My gender played a role in so many facets of life, that it began to feel natural. Embedded. Traditional. The way things are.

I was honestly fine with the way things were and even blissfully unaware of any inequality until I was sexually assaulted at a young age, and then blamed for the assault. Unfortunately, sexual assault and rape happened to me several times in my young life, starting with what seemed to be an innocent prank. I remember I must have been no older than six. I went to a private Episcopal school in Tucson, AZ. that catered to children in kindergarten through eighth grade. This was a little before the school transitioned into an educational institution that helped children with special-needs. Regardless, I was a new student there and one afternoon my class was taken to a nearby park to play. I was cornered by several of my classmates, both young girls and boys, and stripped of all my clothing. The kids took my clothes and ran away, leaving me naked in the park. Scared to death, I climbed up a tree and yelled for help. My mom had always called me "monkey girl" because I could climb just about anything. I used this skill then, seeking protection in the bare tree branches. One of the Episcopal sisters heard my screaming, came over to where I was and looked up at me in the tree. She asked me why I was naked. I explained through my tears that the kids took my clothes. To this day, I can remember holding onto that tree, and feeling the bark scratch my bare skin. However, I can't

9

quite remember her exact words. I do recall distinctly how her words stung, as if I had climbed into a beehive. I remember how my heart felt and how I was horrified.... ashamed. I also remember quite clearly that I was left there, naked in the tree, left to my own thoughts about what I had done wrong. It was made very clear to me that this was my fault. I had been bad. Indeed, being naked was bad. Allowing others to strip me was bad ... As if I had a choice. But... had I done wrong? What had I done to deserve such punishment, my adult self asks today? About ten minutes later, I was presented with a towel, and taken down from the tree. When we got back to the classroom, I was placed in the corner to think about things. Afterward, nobody said anything, and it wasn't even reported to my parents. The silence made things even worse for me. I sat around for days, a lifetime, wondering what the hell I did wrong. Wondering why I was put in the corner, and not the kids that held me down and stripped me. It was quite clear that I was meant to be ashamed and I was meant to feel shame. Indeed, if memory serves me correctly, all the girls were given lessons about shame and modesty, what the school's expectations were for female behavior. Girls walked; boys ran. Girls wore dresses; boys wore pants. Girls played jacks; boys had sports: "Becky, we don't play with lizards... are you trying to be a boy?" Often the girls and boys were separated at school, and when we walked the Stations of the Cross, the girls dressed in pretty white dresses and lined up behind the boys. Girls were always second, obedient, and "proper" in all things. These actions were typical and traditional, genderism embedded in social functions, power relations, and assumptions; they were lessons about how the female gender was second-class. When all was said and done, I did not last long at that school. I was enrolled at Kino Learning Center, a school that better appealed to my personal temperament, and my family's value system.

It is not simply educational environments that promote genderism, but also everyday life. A world filled with accidental, passive-aggressive modes of misogyny and inequality. I can't tell you how often I am told that genderism doesn't exist. I can't tell you how often I am told that sexism doesn't exist by men specifically. Although I am absolutely certain that there are many women who feel this way as well; this statement, this assertion of absolute gender equality is normally given to me by men, young and old: "What are women always complaining about? They have equal rights. Say, go fetch me a beer, will ya?" As far as many are concerned, the great gender gap that was experienced in the 50s, and 60s, and even 70s, has now closed. Don't women work alongside men now? Don't women have the opportunity to earn a paycheck? Didn't a woman run for the presidency? Can't a woman go out and buy a dildo, I mean if she really wants one, let her buy it! Sometimes the assertion of gender equality comes within the "equal...but different" clause, a frame decidedly unequal. Because sexism is an embedded reality within our society, and also societies outside the bounds of the Western world, it doesn't seem wrong... It seems normal. Equal but different seems natural. We rationalize this normality through the gendering of the sexes: Women are weaker than men (evidence: they wear dresses). Women have children, and therefore they must care for these children (evidence: women get pregnant, not men). Women are maternal, better equipped to care for children (evidence: men work outside of the home to provide for their family ... ah, the great food hunt on Wall Street). Women are hard wired to be soft, while men are hard wired to be naturally assertive (evidence: boobs). If men were designed to follow, they would have estrogen rather than testosterone (evidence: a man has a penis!) ... and so on and so forth. However the "equal but different" rationale is a bad joke as well.

Why did the diaphragm slide across the road in the rain?
It's slippery when wet. #birthcontrol #joke

If it is indeed my "lady bits" that are responsible for my unequal position in this world, then I want to understand these so-called "bits" and their powerful effects over a population. Indeed, I have spent a lifetime trying to comprehend the motivation behind linking my lady bits to the different power relationships I encounter in life. I want to know why having breasts, and whether those breasts are firm and unaffected by gravity and aging, should influence my paycheck. Not only am I curious about my experience, I am curious about other women's experiences as well, and whether there are any common intersections that can be found and shared. As such, this memoir is not strictly a memoir in the traditional sense. I only use my personal experiences as a launching pad in order to investigate a diverse community and a collective experience of female sexuality, reproductive knowledge, the use of birth control, and the topic of sexual abuse. Developed from a one-woman stage play, *Writing the Diaphragm Blues* traces female sexuality and gender from childhood to menopause, using critical analysis, as well as humorous theatrical movements, while exploring a personal and a public understanding of sexuality.

In order to extend personal reminiscences into a public forum, this work connects personal memories regarding growing up and sexuality to a wider public discussion found in the news and on the Internet, uncovering interconnected narratives among strangers on topics such as: where babies come from, birth control failures, reproductive knowledge, bouncing boobies, silence regarding sexual assault, image and aging, sex and politics, as well as sluts and crones. I pull on a variety of sources to find this collective dance, including news articles, scholarly articles, Twitter feeds, Facebook updates, public discussion posts, blogs, and YouTube.

Why did the diaphragm cross the road?
It didn't want to commit spermicide. #birthcontrol #joke

Writing the Diaphragm Blues and other Sexual Cacophonies explores feminism, reproductive rights, and sexuality, asking why these topics are continuously distorted and challenged in our modern society. Why do politicians constantly want to play heads or tails with my diaphragm? Why can't we talk about sex in mixed company? Indeed, why did the diaphragm really cross the road? In chapter one, "Eyeballing It" I look at the first moment I became aware of sexuality and the world of reproduction: where do babies come from anyway? Because a person's first memory regarding sexuality can influence his or her understanding about their place in the wider world of sex and gender relations, it is important to approach this topic with foresight, care, and honesty when explaining the facts of life to our children. Yet in American culture, this rarely occurs. From being told by my young peers that babies come from pumpkin seeds, to later finding out that my mom's first sexual memory was of rape, I trace the seeds of sexual mythology to the larger problems of sexual ignorance and sexual assault in American society: babies come from pumpkin seeds, and women mean "yes" when they say "no." This investigation leads to YouTube where the question of where babies come from has been answered many times, and most often, problematically.

From childhood, to adolescence and young adulthood, in chapter two, "The Diaphragm Blues" I ask the reader to come along with me as I recount my journey toward birth control, my first female exam, and being fitted with a diaphragm. I parallel my birth control journey with the pilgrimage of Planned Parenthood's founder Margaret Sanger, and her efforts to make family planning part of the American dream. Both roads were bumpy and littered with mystery, intrigue, legalities and farce.

Chapter three starts out by looking at one of the first jokes my nephew and I learned as children:

ME

Kiddo, what's under there?

NEPHEW

Under where?

ME

Ha, ha, I just made you say underwear!

From childhood jokes about underwear, to lingerie commercials, to the suggestion that a woman asks to be raped because of her fashion choices, "Would a Slut by any Other Name Still Wear Stilettos?" follows my personal experience of sexual assault and rape, and how I was subjected to "victim blaming" in seventh grade because I was not wearing a bra at the time of my assault. Taking back the power of the so-called slut, I also recount my experience at SlutWalk (a new social/political movement rejecting the norm of victim blaming in relation to sexual assault) in Seattle, where I was able to unite with a large community of people all sharing similar experiences, seeking individual and collective restoration of power.

The power to control one's life and one's livelihood is found in many places, but for women, one important place this control is found is through the responsible use of birth control. Originally published with the digital magazine *Harlot: A Revealing Look at the Art of Persuasion* in 2009, chapter four asks the following question: why do politicians and so-called members of "gentlemanly" society want to play heads and tails with a woman's diaphragm? This chapter is an interlude dream of sorts, where I have the opportunity to debate with the likes of John McCain, Hélène Cixous, The Marx Brothers, and other figures in an attempt to understand historic and current rhetoric behind Viagra-centric ethics.

Just as one hopes to achieve when taking Viagra, certain topics about one's sexuality have a moan worthy quality about them, including boobies and orgasms. I share my own moan worthy events in life, from theatre work portraying a prostitute who loves to give women orgasms, *The Vagina Monologues*, to real life moan worthy moments, including being saddled with the name "one-boob Becky" for much of my youth. In this chapter, the Marx Brothers make one of many appearances as my fictional gynecologists and booby surveyors; mirroring the surreal environment of American culture, and its inability to deal with issues of sexuality directly or sensibly. Talk about an inability to deal, here is another diaphragm joke:

What happened when the diaphragm tried to cross the road?
It got lost. #birthcontrol #joke

Okay, the joke may not be all that funny, but I dare readers not to laugh while reading how I lost my diaphragm one time after having sex. Egad! Chapter six examines what would happen if we all lost our diaphragms, and all forms of birth control, to political posturing in an egoist's attempt to saddle society with one ethic, and one point of view regarding birth control. "Losing my Diaphragm" specifically examines ethics in relation to the birth control debate and whether politics or religion has a place in a woman's decision to use or not use birth control. Although humorous, this chapter critically challenges current political rhetoric around birth control, including: Rush Limbaugh's use of the term slut in relation to women who use birth control, Stephen Colbert's humorous claim that male birth control would promote promiscuity within the male population, and America's historic ethical sensibilities regarding the use and existence of contraception. Ultimately, this chapter asks: how can we as a society escape our own egoist attitude about sexuality and reproductive health, moving to a more utilitarian approach of reproductive policy and sensibility?

15

The final chapter of this work, "Mental Pause" examines the traditions and discourses about menopause, and how mythology and the medical community discourage woman-to-woman transmission of information and knowledge about the so-called "change." I recount my mom's journey into menopause, her discovery of horse pee from pregnant mares, and how I had to help her navigate the menopausal road with little information or community support. Now in perimenopause myself, I am curious and flabbergasted by the different effects of social aging, menopause, and self-image as they are communicated via medical, social, and advertising influences in America. What's a woman to do when she gets old? Join a roller derby team!

Why did the diaphragm cross the road?
To cover more ground. #birthcontrol #joke

I would like to end this introduction by thanking several people who all helped make this book a reality. First, I want to thank several friends who were all brave enough to share with me, and you dear reader, their most secret and embarrassing life moments with regard to sex and sexuality: Daniella G., Julia H., Beth K., Jolie C.P., Christy A. W., Alexandra C., KD, Kelly W., Amy G., Rachel M., Amber, Frank N.C., and Ilene M. You are all amazing, bold, and daring people and I appreciate everything you shared for the sake of this book. I must also thank Planned Parenthood, Rollins College, Margaret Sanger, and all the people and events that prompted me to write the original play, which became the groundwork and inspiration for this book. I would also like to thank my family for their love and support. Thank you to my supportive husband George, who kindly listens to me as I yell about Viagra politics and sexism, and who also edits for me, catching my dyslexic eccentricities. I especially appreciate the fact that he can stand me talking about using my diaphragm in public without falling to pieces. I would also like to thank my sister, Deborah, her life partner, Emily, and my dear nephew for offering support and inspiration. Thanks are also extended to my father Fred ("Fred-Dad" throughout this work), who encouraged me and took it in stride that his daughter intended to tell the world about her sexual journey. And I must also thank my mom, k. Margaret Grossman and my stepfather Lee Grossman ("Lee-Dad" throughout this work), for their love and support. Although they no longer walk this earth with the rest of us, they helped create who I am and my values in life. And thanks Lee-Dad for NOT purchasing the chastity belt as you so threatened. Dear and long time friends Art Dumaplin and Amy Lawson Yamamoto collaborated on the cover for the book and both were gracious with my numerous requests for small changes here and there! Art is responsible for coming up with the artwork and Amy took care of the text design.[2] They both came to my rescue and I am so grateful! I also wish to offer a very special thank you to my dear friend and editor Kathryn D. Ketrenos. I have known Kathryn since high school, and after becoming reacquainted on Facebook, she was kind enough to offer me her services as an editor. I am not sure she knew what she was signing up for, but she has turned out to be a fantastic editor, pushing me as a writer and a thinker. For this I am truly grateful! Finally, I want to thank all those people who have influenced my life, leading me to this place and all the memories I have to pull from; I would be incomplete without each and every one of you.

---

[2] Images chosen for cover art are copyright free.

Continuous Conversations: Where Babies Come From

I asked my friends: How did you find out where babies came from? The answers were all over the board!

As far back as I can remember, I have known the truth about where babies come from. Knowing my mother, I am pretty sure we were told the truth early on.
    -- Julia H.

You know, I don't honestly remember having this conversation. I do remember asking my mother what a period was and she told me to talk to my sister about it. My sister was 7 years older and I guess better equipped to discuss this type of thing with me.
    -- Beth K.

I don't remember being told by anyone where babies come from. I knew little sister came from Mommy's tummy, and I figured out somehow it got there with the help of Daddy's baby stick.
    -- Jolie CP

When I was in third grade a "friend" had been spreading a vicious rumor saying that I raped a first grader in my neighborhood. I didn't even know what raped meant, but could tell that it was bad, so I asked my dad. My dad then explained what intercourse was, what rape was, and the birds and the bees which left me even more upset that someone was telling people that I had done this horrific thing.

-- Rachel M.

Older playground kids told me. I was under the impression that there was some sort of docking mechanism and was shocked and frightened to learn as a teen that the penis went INSIDE the vagina. It made condoms make a lot more sense though.

-- Alexandra C

I was put in front of a TV with a cartoon movie from the library and that is how I learned the [gist] of it.

-- Amber

From my dad, the stork brought you.

-- Ilene M.

Eyeballing It

My mother's first memory of life was rape. My sister and I did not know this for many years, although there were signs all around. The biggest sign being that of an eyeball. Mom often drew beautiful and detailed eyes on napkins, scraps of paper, or indented into the surface of soft clay. When my sister or I would ask her what it meant, she would tell us:

"It's to remind you that Mommy's always watching! She has eyes everywhere!"

Or

"It is the sign of the great Egyptian God Ra; the all seeing and watching God of the universe!"

"Is he like Santa Claus?"

"Yes!" She beamed. "But Ra's gift is the gift of life, not rocking horses."

I started drawing eyes too. I enjoyed sketching almond shaped eyes, although I disliked the nut as a child. I would draw two lines over the top of the eye, one line for the crease of the eyelid and the other for the eyebrow. A long crease would follow from the eyebrow down to form the nose. But unlike my mom, I graduated from drawing one solitary eye, to two eyes that would look back at you from the page.

Writing this memory down, I sit and wonder what my mom must have felt or thought with my imitation of her eye drawings, for I now know this was her first memory, and her attacker's eye was what she focused on while being raped. She was a very young child when it first happened. This sexual abuse would follow her throughout her childhood, adolescence, and into the throes of young adulthood. Much of it stopped at thirteen or fourteen when she pulled a gun on her attacker, her stepfather, and hitchhiked out of Fairbanks, Alaska, taking to the Alcan Highway for escape. Maybe she viewed the single eye not only as a physical example of her attacker, but the all-seeing Ra, a universal God waiting to pass judgment when we pass from the world of the living, into the world of the dead. It is conjecture on my part, but not out of the ballpark of possibilities, considering her way of thinking. Mom believed in covering her tracks, and she was open to many spiritual traditions. Right before she died, Mom had me fetch a Priest, a Rabbi and, if I could have located one in time, she would have also appreciated a Buddhist Monk to help her transition into the next reality. Knowing that Mom enjoyed the mystery embedded in many metaphysical beliefs, she might have hoped the eye acted as a Total Recall "Ra" device, which recorded all events occurring in her life. Anubis, the Jackal God of death and a consumer of evil souls, could then review these recordings. The owners of the human eye(s) would be sentenced when the list of histories were told, and the scales of Ma'at deemed them criminal and unworthy. Their eyes would be plucked and fried for pre-game treats, served with beer. Justice would then be had as Ammut devoured their souls. The eye may take and it may give as well. The truth is, I have no idea what she thought or felt when she drew her many eyes, but she was drawing them up to the time of her death, at 54 years of age.

My first memory is of laughter and love, but my first sexual memory is of rape. A relative raped my sister and me. We were also both sexually violated by men/boys inside and outside of our "family." How can one fight a legacy of such betrayal? I would like to say that our experiences, my mom, my sister, and my own were unique. The fact is simple, sexual abuse, in all its diverse forms, is much more common than often thought. According to RAINN (Rape, Abuse, and Incest National Network), 1 in 6 females will be sexually assaulted, whereas 1 in 33 men will experience the same.[3] George Mason University Sexual Assault Services estimate is even more frightening, arguing that 1 in 3 females in the United States are raped.[4] Even with the disparity between the figures, it is clear sexual abuse is common rather than rare. For those who endure and survive sexual abuse, the trick is how to be something other than a victim, and how to avoid being defined merely as a survivor. The hope is to be able to relate to and enjoy sex in a healthy way, and to be defined by the life we lead, not the rape survived. My mom, herself without emotional or physical support, wanted to offer her children what she did not have, a healthy view and understanding of sex. Sadly, her rapes haunted her until death, but they did not define her. To her daughters she gave the greatest gift she could give, the lesson of how to be defined by life, not sex, sexual designation, or sexual assault.

From a very early age, Mom spoke frankly about sex. As she explained to her daughters, sexual mythology and sexual lies are fodder for ignorance, genderism, and sexual assault. I remember coming home from kindergarten with the misconception that babies were delivered to new mommies and daddies via the stork, possibly the same stork related to the Vlasic pickle stork. It seemed reasonable to my young mind. Maybe after the pickle season was concluded, the storks picked up extra cash by delivering babies. My parents always had part-time jobs ... so? Regardless, I had this information on

---

[3] "Statistics." *Rape, Abuse, and Incest National Network.* ND. 2009. Web. 3 July 2011.
[4] George Mason University Sexual Assault Services. "Worldwide Sexual Assault Statistics." *George Mason University.* 2005. Web. 3 July 2011.

the storks' divine profession given to me by a very reliable source, another kindergartner. Around Halloween I was also told, by an even more reliable kindergartner, that babies started out as pumpkin seeds then, when the baby was ready, the stork delivered it. The stork information did not bother me, but this new information about the seeds ... this horrified me deeply. After all, there were times I accidentally ate seeds. When I had oranges and watermelon. A seed is a seed, right? So, what happened to all those seeds? All those potential babies? Then there was something far worse: my mom baked pumpkin seeds, with a healthy dose of salt, to eat after carving our pumpkins. To this day I remember watching Mom that faithful October, after we had carved our pumpkins for Halloween, putting a pan of salt covered pumpkin seeds into the oven and turning on the heat. I cried, deeply and fearfully! I yelled for her to stop killing babies: What on earth was she doing?[5]

"Honey, what are you talking about? I am making a treat for us," she reasoned.

"You are killing babies! Stop it!"

"What? I am doing no such thing. These are just seeds. Where in the hell did you hear such a thing?"

"Bobby's mom told him that babies came from pumpkins! So the seeds are little babies."[6]

It is important to understand that Mom was a young woman who had me at nineteen. She was an idealist, a hippy, and a frank woman who believed honesty was the best policy when raising children. Both Mom and Fred-Dad were appalled that a parent would tell his or her child babies came from pumpkin seeds. Can you imagine? Today, the adult in me creates a science fiction version of this story where a machine

---

[5] This may be how horror stories regarding "pod people" got developed - movie fans delight!

[6] Honestly, I cannot remember the young boy's name, but Bobby will do.

like umbilical cord/pumpkin vine pumps life into palpitating pumpkins that harbor all those seeds. To add to this fiction, the character Linus, from the popular comic strip and *Peanuts* movies, and his Great Pumpkin are likely real. Indeed, "The Great Pumpkin" God comes and douses each round orange fruit with souls before the harvest, we have to account for twins after all, and if seeds equal fetuses in this equation, then one could see fifty souls or so per pumpkin. Later, the seeds are extracted by millions of potential parents around the globe, who, scooping them out, swallow the seeds whole and hope that one or more will take root. They then carve the leftover pumpkin in honor of the Great Pumpkin God, a ritual accompanied by the eating of candy, a child's favorite treat, and the celebration of souls. This is all done around Halloween, of course, which is why there are more babies born in July than any other month. Wait, I was born in July ... hmm.

On Facebook, I read a status update that my nephew was told by a friend that babies come from the great baby cloud. Since cloud computing is getting so very popular, I could not help but imagine Google being behind this operation, talk about Google+, with Apple on its heels for iTunes downloads. Picture this, baby souls stored in "the cloud," being pumped with information from the Internet - Twitter feeds the virtual soul fetus along with Facebook wall updates, and targeted advertisements. Advertisers would be in heaven! Consider the potential of training a child to be a consumer even before he or she popped out of the womb! Capital delight!

If I had been growing up at this time in society, I might have associated the baby cloud theory with cloud computing, but I had pumpkin seeds; lovely, and rather delicious, pumpkin seeds. When my mom saw me throw a fit over her making a treat for us all, she was flabbergasted. Being the woman that she was, she would have none of these lies. She marched to the local bookstore and picked up a book that explained where babies come from in a simple but straightforward way. I no longer remember the title, but I do remember the "ah-ha" moment I had as I read the book and Mom explained things to me in a rational, appropriate way. There were pictures and stories about how a man and a woman would become close physically and make a baby, which then developed in the mommy's belly until it was ready to be born into the world. My mom, being a writer herself, believed in books and the power of books. She proved time and time again that you could learn anything you needed to from a book, and so she relied on a book to help her tell the story. I liked the story so much, I brought the book to class for "show-and-tell": I showed and told. I got in trouble, and not for the last time in my life.

People are so weird about sex. We have been doing it since the beginning of time, and yet we are not to talk about it in "mixed" company. Although I am not clear on what or who constitutes mixed company, I am crystal clear that it is not okay for a kindergartner to bring a book about where babies come from to class, and set her classmates straight. It is fine, however, to tell children that babies come from storks, pumpkins, or clouds. I had set Bobby and several of my classmates straight on the whole "baby thing" during the show-and-tell portion of class. Show-and-tell came after story time in my class and took up a good portion of the end of the school day.[7] By this time of day, my teacher, a young woman who dressed herself to look like she was fifteen years older than she actually was, my mom's observation, would zone out and develop the "K-Mart" stare; you know, that glossy look we often get when shopping in K-Marts, Wal-Marts and other stores as our carts mysteriously fill up with unneeded goods. I got halfway through the book on where babies come from before my teacher "came-to" and realized what was happening. She told me to sit down. My book was confiscated.

---

[7] This is a grade-school ritual where children show something important to their class and talk about it.

25

My mom did not know I took the book to class, or that I intended to educate my classmates. When she was called about the incident, and told how outraged many parents were about the book and the factual information disseminated to their kids, she was not mad, but proud of me.

"Listen Principle Houser,[8] my daughter came home the other day with the misconception that babies come from pumpkins."

"Yes, Mrs. McCarthy, we are not talking about pumpkins."

"Yes we are. I am saying that a kid in her class at YOUR school was told by his mother that kids come from pumpkins, and during Halloween."

"What's the point?"

"The point is simple, I was baking pumpkin seeds that day. Can you imagine what happened? What the hell was that mother thinking, telling her kid such bullshit. It is enough to screw a kid up for life."

"The point is, Mrs. McCarthy, it is not your child's place to be telling the other children in her class about the finer points of sex and birth."

"What the fuck do you call the pumpkin story? (With irritation) Let me get this straight, Mr. Houser, myths are okay to spread but the truth is forbidden?"

"Parents are upset and I am asking you to talk to your daughter about what is appropriate and not appropriate to say to her classmates."

"She did say the appropriate thing Mr. Houser, she told the truth. You need more kids like her, asshole."

I told you my mom was frank, didn't I? The concept of "appropriate behavior" was very important to Mom; I cannot tell you how many times in my life I heard this phrase:

"Rebecca, was that appropriate behavior you just demonstrated?"

---

[8] Again, I do not remember the principle's name, but Houser sounds as good as any, and it sets the right tone.

26

"Ah ... No? Sorry Mom."

"Don't say sorry to me, say sorry to that poor girl with half her hair shaved off! For Christ sake, what were you thinking child?"

Regarding the appropriateness of this situation, the logic for Mom was simple: how can you have truthful upright citizens if you raise children with lies about important things such as "where do babies come from?" If we think about it, she is right. Consider the myriad myths about sex that lead to frightening consequences, such as unwanted pregnancy, abortion, rape and abandonment of children by their parents:

- You cannot get pregnant the first time; a body new to sex will reject sperm.
- It takes more than having sex one time to get a sexually transmitted disease.
- You can get pregnant if you sit on a toilet seat where sperm was left.
- You can't get pregnant if you have sex during your period.
- You can't get pregnant if he pulls out really fast, before he ejaculates *all* the way.
- It is not my fault she is pregnant; SHE forgot her pill.
- She said "no," but what she really meant was "yes."
- "If it's legitimate rape, the female body has ways to try to shut that whole thing down."[9]

---

[9] This mythology was proclaimed as truth by Missouri Congressman Todd Akin, while being interviewed about his no-exceptions opposition to abortion on a Fox affiliate news station in St. Louis, KTVI-TV, August 19 2012. However, in 1988, Rep. Stephen Freind (R. PA.) proclaimed a similar myth about rape victims being able to avoid getting pregnant: "A woman secrets a certain secretion, which has the tendency to kill sperm." See: Baer, John M. "Freind's Rape-Pregnancy Theory Refuted. *Philly.com.* 23 March 2012. Web. 28 August 2012.

- Holding hands is a "gateway sexual activity."[10]
- Having an abortion will give you breast cancer.[11]
- It is likely that statutory rape or incest will not cause pregnancy.[12]

Indeed, our unwillingness to speak frankly about sex is what gets many of us into trouble. Misinformation, mythology, and misguidance all unite to spell catastrophe. There is the myth, for example, that rape is sexy. Anne Rice, an author I enjoy, writes how women long for a type of "sex," to be forcefully taken and devoured by some character's thick and ready organ. In this case, the rapist was a spirit named Lasher in her famous series on the Mayfair Witches. Rice is not the only author to make this claim, since romance novels repeatedly present forceful sex as a secret desire harbored by women. We never hear the more responsible version, for example:

> Joan and Bob looked at each other longingly and with great expectation. Bob was in fine form tonight. He had walked into the club and grabbed Joan by the arm with just enough force that it hurt, but in a good way. Joan had almost smiled and giggled; almost broken character.

---

[10] Tennessee lawmakers in 2012 concocted this mythical gem, senate bill 3310. See: NA. "Tennessee Sex Education Bill Promotes Abstinence-Only, Warns against 'Gateway Sexual Activity." *Huffington Post*. 23 July 2012. Web. 28 August 2012.

[11] This unsupported medical myth exists in an anti-abortion law passed by the Kansas House of Representatives. See: Celock, John. "Kansas Abortion Bill: Lawmakers Pass Sweeping Measure." *Huffington Post*. 4 May 2012. Web. 28 August 2012.

[12] Recently suggested by Steve King (R-Iowa). See: Bennett, Dashiell. "Steve King Never Heard of Anyone Getting Pregnant by Statutory Rape." *The Atlantic Wire*. 21 August 2012. Web. 28 August 2012.

"I know you want it lady, I can smell want all over your body." This was a new line that Bob had been working on, and although Joan was not sure how "want" smelled, she enjoyed the passion that Bob delivered the line with.

"No. Let me go. I don't know who the hell you are. Please, I will scream, I swear!" Joan replied on cue. Joan and Bob had a mature and trusting sexual relationship that allowed them to freely game play. One of Bob's favorite role-playing games was a mock version of rape between two strangers meeting in a dance club. Joan didn't mind this game either because it was total fantasy. Besides, Bob and Joan had a "safe" word that they used when things got out of hand.

What a buzz kill, right? Indeed, there is nothing like the use of explanatory language to kill sexual tension. God forbid we present sexual tastes in a more realistic and responsible light. But Rice is only borrowing from a culture that has perpetuated the "rape is fun" myth. In fact, it was Anne Rice's Facebook feed where I read about a recent LGBT, "Gay Day" celebration protest in Grand Rapids, Michigan.[13] Here, the protestors, all holding Bibles, yelled at the women participating, telling them to "keep your pussy clean" and watch out because they would be raped, and enjoy it:

"Back in the day there was no free power, there was no going to the mall," one protester tells the woman. "There was, 'sit your ass in this house until I bring my ass home.' And if your ass get to going out there like you said, guess

---

[13] I have found Anne Rice's Facebook feed to be one of the most "activist" and fully interactive social media feeds promoting religious freedom, woman's rights, sexual equality, and a voice for victims of sexual assault. The author is also fully interactive with her Facebook audience, a rare thing indeed.

what?" a second protester adds. "You get raped. And that's what's going to happen to you. … Keep your pussy clean, that's all you need to do. Do you understand?" After one man claims, "the Lord said that," the woman challenges him to find the corresponding Bible verse. He responds with Isaiah 13: "'their children also shall be dashed to pieces before their eyes; their houses shall be spoiled, and their wives ravished. 'What does 'ravished' mean? It means, we going to rape your ass," the protester explains. *"And I'm going to have fun doing that shit. And you going to like that. I promise you."* (Emphasis added)[14]

How can we be surprised at this line of reasoning when much of our cultural understanding about sexuality, sexual relations, and gender stems from poorly constructed mythology? We hear this same line of reckoning everywhere, and there are even popular songs and popular artists that celebrate the raping of women, who, we are assured, will enjoy the experience: Bitches like being "turned out." This was rapper Too Short's line of reasoning when, for a column in XXL, he offered his so-called "fatherly" advise to young men:

When you get to late middle school, early high school and you start feeling a certain way about the girls... I'm gonna tell you a couple tricks... A lot of the boys are going to be running around trying to get kisses from the girls... We're going way past that. I'm taking you to the hole... You push her up against the wall... You take your finger and put a

---

[14] Edwards, David. "Man with Bible threatens to rape woman during 'Gay Day' in Michigan." *The Raw Story*. 9 August 2012. Web. 9 August 2012.

little spit on it and you stick your finger in her underwear and you rub it on there and watch what happens.[15]

The phrase "turn out," as in to "turn a girl out," maintains a variety of definitions including "a hoe's first outing" (sexual encounter), to making a young girl a prostitute, to forcing a homosexual encounter, or changing one's sexual orientation via force and influence during a sexual encounter.[16] Most of the definitions contain this idea of forcing oneself on another, which can be seen in rapper Too Short's suggestion that you push a girl up against the wall, trapping her there while you wet your finger and slip it into her underwear. Sexual force. The idea is to overpower the person in question and take control – take what you want. This is why some political movements see sex and rape as a viable weapon of war. Rape, after all, is not really about sex as much as it is about power, and making the victim an object to be conquered and controlled, rather than a human being to be seen and understood. Sexual myths and lies lead to horrible consequences. Yet this is what most of our society puts forth by keeping silent about sex, when offering the bottom line of "just say no," or telling our children that babies come from pumpkin seeds and baby clouds. Indeed, I refused to eat pumpkin seeds for years ... such a shame, really.

I was curious as to whether the pumpkin seed story was a strange one-time occurrence in my kindergarten class, or maybe a wider known lie disseminated to the general population. Thank God for the Internet! After doing a quick and dirty Google search, using the search term of "babies come from pumpkin seeds," I found that this myth was undeniably widespread. At one website, I learned how a mom

---

[15] Ramsey. Donovan X. "Rapper Too Short, in XXL Column, Gives Boys Advice to 'Turn Girls Out.'" *The Grio.* 14 February 2012. Web. 7 March 2012.

[16] NA. "Turn out." *Urban Dictionary.* ND. Web. 7 August 2012.

and dad go to a pumpkin patch where the father picks up a pumpkin seed and gives it to the mother to swallow. Soon after, a doctor unzips the mother's tummy in order to get the baby out.[17] From a site called the *Wedding Bee Boards*, a message board entry on "Where Do Babies Come From," there were a few seed stories.[18] *CorgiTales*, on 26 February 2011, wrote:

> Okay no joke ... I'm going to tell you what my parents told me when I was little. It made perfect sense at the time and I could not figure out why my older cousins kept asking me to explain it and then giggling! 'When a man and a woman are in love and are married to each other, they pray to God for a baby. Then when a woman eats something with seeds like an orange or a watermelon, God turns the seed into a baby!' lies ... all lies .... :)

Honeybear wrote that her "best friend's [sic] parents told her that her mom swallowed a pumpkin seed!" *Sage* continued the seed mythology with a new explanation for the function of the bellybutton: "My parents told me a bunch of garbage about 'planting a seed' so I took it literally and thought that during the wedding, a man put a seed in the woman's belly button and then she was pregnant. I had a pretty vivid imagination, though ;)." At least I was not alone! There were several other people given a "seed" story, whether pumpkin, watermelon or orange, as an explanation to the age-old question. After my initial search, I wanted to take my inquiry a bit further because, I thought to myself, if I was a young kid wondering where babies come from, and I wanted to find out without having to ask an adult, where would I go? YouTube ... but of course!

---

[17] "Where Do Babies Come From." *Stupid-free.Livejournal.com*. 29 September 2008. Web. 3 July 2011.
[18] "Where Do Babies Come From?" *WeddingBee.com*. 12 December 2009. Web. 3 July 2011.

I searched YouTube using the phrase "Where do babies come from," and came away with a rather disturbing array of videos on the topic. Judging from the top videos returned to me on my YouTube search, you do not want to go to YouTube to find an answer to this question! The top videos I viewed offered nothing but misinformation, as well as a warped presentation regarding women's role in the baby making process. Often in these videos, a woman is presented as nothing more than a passive participant in the process of birth, being little more than a human incubator. The first video I came across was posted by *1lovethewkuk* in May of 2007. This video is meant to be a small comedy skit between a father and a son. At the time of my viewing, the video had been seen 629,422 times, and had received 3,311 likes and only 57 dislikes.

Where Do Babies Come From

Scene: At a park bench.

(The scene opens with two guys, one adult and the other a child, sitting on a park bench.)

SON
Dad, where do babies come from?

FATHER
Well ah, from inside your wiener.

SON
What?

FATHER
Inside your wiener are all these little eggs.

SON

That's gross.

FATHER

Yep, it's pretty gross.

SON

Yeah. Well how does that turn into a baby?

FATHER

Well, you find yourself a girl and you put your wiener in her and then you squish all your eggs out.

SON

Well ... er ... do you like pee in her?

FATHER

Yep. Then the eggs grow into babies and she pushes them out.

SON

Like with her poop?

FATHER

Yeah. Pretty much.

SON

Well if she doesn't push them out, will the babies get too big and crawl out of her mouth?

FATHER

Probably. Geeze I never thought about that.

SON

Well, what do babies eat when they first come out?

FATHER

Ah ... boobs.

SON

Did I eat boobs?

FATHER

Yep.

SON

Gross.

FATHER

Yeah, it's pretty gross.

SON

So you have eggs inside of your wiener, and you pee them in a girl, and then that turns into a baby, and then she poops them out, and then it eats boobs.

FATHER

Yep, that's about it.

SON

My real Dad says he doesn't want me coming to the park and talking to you anymore.

FATHER

That's okay; I'm really not supposed to be hanging out with little kids anyway.[19]

This was the very first video that came up on YouTube with my search, and if I was a young kid looking to find out

---

[19] Ilovethewkuk. "Where Do Babies Come From?" YouTube. 12 May 2007. Web. 3 July 2011.

about biology, I would likely come away more confused, not to mention a bit horrified (women get peed into and then poop out babies?!). I am aware that this is a comic video; I am also aware that all forms of discourse send messages about how we should think on a variety of topics. Viral videos that grace our Facebook pages, Twitter feeds, YouTube viewings, emails and so on are of particular influence in our modern world. According to Warnick and Heineman, two leading experts in the world of digital rhetoric, a viral video is one that receives a lot of views in a short period of time, generates several responses, and relies on pathos (an appeal to our emotions), as well as novelty (63-64).[20] Viral videos are interesting because the videos, the embedded values and information in the video spread a lot like a virus. Specifically, Warnick and Heineman point to the concept of rhizomatic travel, that is traveling "horizontally, with many points of connection and departure" (65). Rhizome is a term that means "mass of roots" in Ancient Greek, and in botany the rhizome refers to plant stems that sends out various shoots. Once broken up, each root can give life to a new plant allowing for endless reproduction. As Warnick and Heineman point out in *Rhetoric Online*, Guy Geleuze and Félix Guattari first borrowed the term and image of the rhizome in 1972 because it was a useful image in examine the dissemination of language and values, for their discussion regarding capitalism.[21] The key here is endless reproduction of ideals, information, and ethics; this is reproduction that can reinforce misinformation in our society. One major piece of misinformation being spread by the above-mentioned viral video on reproduction, as well as

---

[20] Warnick, Barbara, and David S. Heineman. "Circulation and Rhetorical Uptake: Viral Video and Internet Memes." *Rhetoric Online: The Politics of New Media.* 2nd Ed. New York: Peter Lang, 2012. Pp. 62-74. Print.

[21] See: Deleuze, Gilles, and Félix Guattari. *A Thousand Plateaus: Capitalism and Schizophrenia.* London, u.a.: Continuum, 2008. Print.

many others like it, is this idea that a woman is thing to be utilized, rather than a uniquely creative being. What I find of interest between my pumpkin seed story and this viral video "pee" story is that in both versions the woman is nothing more than a passive vessel, a kind of thing really, existing to incubate the potential child in question. Consider this: men "impregnate" women. This also suggests a woman is generally a bystander in the process, while the man is the "active agent" that plants the seed, pees the seed or, in some cases, shoves the seed through a woman's bellybutton.[22] What we have here is seventeenth century scientific logic that has a meme like existence in our society.

The term "meme" can be traced back to the scientist Richard Dawkins:

We need a name for the new replicator, a noun that conveys the idea of a unit of cultural transmission, or a unit of imitation. 'Mimeme' comes from a suitable Greek root, but I want a monosyllable that sounds a bit like 'gene'. I hope my classicist friends will forgive me if I abbreviate mimeme to *meme*. If it is any consolation, it could alternatively be thought of as being related to 'memory', or to the French word *même*. It should be pronounced to rhyme with 'cream'.[23]

Dawkins offers his readers a variety of meme examples such as "tunes, ideas, catch-phrases, clothes fashions, ways of making pots or of building arches."[24] The "woman as bystander and incubator in the reproduction process" is a

---

[22] This seed shoved through the belly button action has got to hurt worse than a piercing; and take it from me, belly button piercings hurt like hell!

[23] Dawkins, Richard. *The Selfish Gene*. Oxford: Oxford University Press, 2006. P. 192. Internet resource.

[24] Ibid.

meme that can be found with the seventeenth century so-called *spermists* who promoted the theory of *homunculus*: the belief that fetuses were fully formed microscopic beings that resided in the sperm sack. When ejaculated into a woman, this humanoid creature would grow inside the womb, aka incubator, until it was ready to be born into the world. This theory was built on the philosophy of pre-formationism: a belief that preceded and stands in opposition to evolution. Pre-formationism argues that all organisms were created at the same time (the beginning of creation) and new generations of organisms are fully formed, but miniature versions that grow into their fully developed forms (height, width, and weight).[25] The homunculus' take on the pre-formationism theory was developed and presented by Nicolaas Hartsoeker in his 1694 publication *Essai de Dioptrique*. Although discredited, because this theory meshed, agreed with cultural assumptions regarding the worth of a woman, it took on meme status as it continued to be discussed in textbooks examining the age-old question: where do babies come from? In *Genetics: An Introduction to the Study of Heredity* (1922), Herbert Eugene Walter writes: "aided by a poor microscope and a good imagination the theory of pre-formation was carried to such an extreme that a manikin or 'homunculus' was actually figured by Hartsoeker seated within the head of a human spermatozoa" (252).[26] Walter could be talking about our first YouTube video in both theory and imagination. Here is a meme from the seventeenth century continuing its rhizomatic transformation as a modern internet meme: "So, you have eggs inside of your wiener, and you pee them in a girl, and

---

[25] Maienschein, Jane. "Epigenesis and Preformationism." *The Stanford Encyclopedia of Philosophy (Fall 2008 Edition)*, Edward N. Zalta (ed.). Web. 3 July 2011.

[26] Walter, Herbert Eugene. *Genetics: An Introduction to the Study of Heredity*. The MacMillan Company of Canada. Toronto: 1922.

then that turns into a baby, and then she poops them out, and then it eats boobs." Oy Vey.

The second viral video on my search list, that also promotes our meme, was a short scene from the movie *Knocked Up*, uploaded by *yummyyanko* on September 22, 2008. At the time of my viewing, it had been seen 221,581 times, garnishing 406 likes, and only 4 dislikes.

Knocked Up

(A family is gathered at the dinner table. A young girl, about eight years old, asks a group of adults where babies come from. Rather than answering, the adults ask her what she thinks.)

LITTLE GIRL

Well, I think a stork ... well he drops it down, and then a hole ... (Pointing to her head) ... goes into your body, and there is blood everywhere, coming out of your head, and then you push your belly button and your butt falls off, and then you hold your butt and you have to dig and you find a little baby. (Girl giggles)

MOTHER

That's exactly right.[27]

Butts are a popular place for babies to depart from during the birthing process. Maybe there are two kinds of babies: butt babies and vagina babies (*Beavis & Butt-Head?*). Regardless, again we have the image of a passive-incubator-machine-woman waiting to receive the makings of a baby. Here, however, we do not need a man to pee into us, but a stork to bring the prize.

---

[27] yummyyanko. "*Knocked-Up*: Where Do Babies Come From." YouTube. 22 September 2008. Web. 3 July 2011.

Storks are also popular memes and have been with us for years regarding the baby delivery business. According to Richard Torregrossa in *Fun Facts about Babies*, stork mythology started out with the ancient Scandinavian observation that these birds nested in chimneys and were monogamous.[28] The modern stork mythology comes to us from Hans Christian Andersen who, in the late nineteenth century, presented the world with the lovely story "The Storks," which explains why all storks are called "Peter" and have the lucrative profession of delivering babies, that is, when they are not manufacturing pickles: "But that good boy—you have not forgotten him, the one who said, 'It is wrong to laugh at animals!'—for him we will bring a brother and a sister too. And as his name is Peter, all of you shall be called Peter too" (153).[29] Kids love Hans Christian Andersen and his stork story, then and now. Indeed, several videos I watched contained a seed of Andersen's story, such as the TV commercial from Kaiser, an ad for Permanente Thrive, advertised as Kaiser's "comprehensive medical approach to health." This video had 31,976 views with only 85 likes, and 2 dislikes. Kaiser interviews children about where they think babies come from. The answers were varied: storks, the hospital, your mom, "something else," hugs, very special hugs, and the "it's complicated" cop-out explanation offered by the adult voice-over for the commercial.[30] The explanation of hugs and "very special" hugs worry me a bit. Children like to hug, a lot. So will telling this story, that babies come from hugs, make our children paranoid to hug? It would have wigged me out.

---

[28] Torregrossa, Richard. *Fun Facts About Babies*. New York: Dell Pub, 1997. P. 18. Print

[29] Anderson, HC, HW. Dulcken, Alfred W. Bayes, Edward Dalziel, and George Dalziel. *Stories for the Household*. London: Routledge, 1866. Print.

[30] Kaiser. "Where Do Babies Come From? (Are You Kidding)." YouTube. 10 August 2010. Web. 3 July 2011.

The fourth viral video was of a little boy who thought babies come from Costco. Yes, buy in bulk! The child's nanny, with the parent's permission, uploaded this clip on May 7th, 2007. It has been viewed 5,454,887 times, and has received 6,236 likes and 1,998 dislikes.[31] The Nanny's video was followed by a teacher's presentation of her class, uploaded by *shortie5149* on December 8, 2007. This video has gotten 18,669 hits with only 38 likes and 1 dislike. Like the first video I witnessed, the egg is said to have first been in the father's stomach, and then, when then the egg grows a certain amount, an angel helps take the egg from the father and puts it into the mother.[32] Brothers of pre-formation-ala-homunculus meme, unite!

The next two videos were formed as comic skits, created and uploaded by men (from what I can tell, all the films on the first results page were created by men except for two videos: babies are from Costco, and the video uploaded by *shortie5149*). *TimothyDeLaGhetto2* films a mock commercial for Welch's Jelly. He explains how there was a commercial contest that he hoped to win. The contest was canceled and so the short film was then posted to YouTube in March of 2009. The video has gotten 309,354 hits with 2,460 likes and 101 dislikes:

Welch's Jelly Contest Ad: Dad, Where Do Babies Come From?

(A Father is making a peanut butter sandwich with grape jelly - the kind you squeeze out of a bottle. His teenage son comes into the kitchen.)

---

[31] jshuffer. "Where Do Babies Come From?" YouTube. 7 May 2007. Web. 3 July 2011.

[32] shortie5149. "Where Do Babies Come From?" YouTube. 8 December 2011. Web. 3 July 2011.

                                   SON
Hey Dad?

                                 FATHER
What?

                                   SON
Where do babies come from? (The grape Jelly Bottle hits the
table with a loud sounding crash.)

                                 FATHER
Come sit here. Well. There's a man and a woman, and they
love each other, and they get married, and they stay together,
and ah ... and they love each other, a man and a woman. And
... so ... so ... they love each other so they stay together, and
that's what happens.

                                   SON
(With a confused look on his face) I don't get it.

                                 FATHER
Well, ok ... (picks up the two halves of his sandwich) ... this is
a man (referring to the sandwich half with peanut butter on it)
... and this is a woman (referring to the sandwich half with
jelly on it) ... and (slapping the two halves together) ... baby!

                                   SON
(Confused son takes sandwich and eats) Oh, ummm. (The
father is suddenly standing naked) Why you naked?

PRODUCT TAG / ANNOUNCER

Welch's. Bringing Families Together. (The tag line, over the author's vanity card) The royal penis is clean your highness." "Thank you - king shit."[33]

What I love about this video is that man stands alone in the birthing *homunculus* process – with no need of a woman to even incubate – she just needs to exist within marriage.[34] At first it may sound as if I am making a giant leap here, but follow the logic for a moment: the father never explains where babies come from specifically, but generally. It takes a "married" Mommy and Daddy, we are told, that decide to stay together; the staying together part is the most important element in this story. To demonstrate the more sticky (pun intended) process of procreation, the father slams two halves of a peanut butter and jelly sandwich together. The two halves become a whole and then the son eats the sandwich – taking it into his body. Next, the video cuts to the father, who is now naked: a fully-grown offspring? Ah, so that's how babies are grown your highness king shit – thank you.

Women are a bit less ignored in the second to the last film I viewed. It was created and posted by *gradualreport* in December 2009. This video has received 51,390 hits with 1,764 likes, and only 39 dislikes. This comedic editorial is presented in the form of a rant:

Where do babies come from? Physically they come from a crevice that bleeds once a month – ugh, that's yucky. Emotionally they come from something entirely different.

---

[33] TimothyDeLaGhetto2. "Where Do Babies Come From?" YouTube. 9 March 2009. Web. 3 July 2011.

[34] I wonder how many of these myths will change with society's acceptance of same sex couples. It will be a relief to be presented with a more socially widen image of "family" and love.

Babies come from a magical beautiful place when two people love each other. Or maybe babies come from an unhealthy co-dependent relationship that the two people involved in mistakenly trick themselves into believing that bringing a child into the relationship will only strengthen it, when in reality it's probably the thing that is going to break it up, because it will force them to realize that they are a bunch of selfish assholes. And the third party is actually a different being spawned from the underlined hatred of the world trying to fuck them out of something they once wanted: "When I had you, I had to give up on my dream." "I was going to be a professional kite-board surfer. And then you were born, and I had to work." Or babies come from rape victims. That's right; victims that have been raped have babies some times. I am not angry ...[35]

We are given three versions of baby creation: one, babies come from a crevice that bleeds once a month. Although one can assume that the author(s) of this video are associating women with bleeding crevices, it is not clearly stated. Indeed, the viewer is not told if this crevice is female or male; hell, it could be a mystical mountain-bleeding crevice for all we know. All we do know is that it bleeds once a month. Second, a dysfunctional couple will use the act of creation to hold a bad relationship together by having a baby. Third, rape. Again, if I was a young person looking for more information on how babies are made and where babies come from, I might leave this video disturbed and seeking professional, psychiatric help. I should note that the *gradualreport* attempted to answer this question twice, and in a second video there is a visual recreation of birth, using a stuffed animal dog named Flopsy. Our host takes Flopsy to get pregnant, but he never explains that portion of the process; rather, we are taken directly to the

---

[35] Gradualreport. "Where Do Babies Come From?" YouTube. 14 December 2009. Web. 3 July 2011.

action scene: the birth. In this case, the bloody crevice is in between the hind legs of Flopsy. Pounding the crevice area, our video star finally punches out a "baby" Flopsy, which is pulled out and born into the world.[36]

The final video I watched was a political viral video urging California citizens to vote yes on Proposition 8. Posted by *yesonprop81025*, this video had 199,095 hits, 3,211 likes and 3,989 dislikes.

Proposition 8: Where Do Babies Come From?

Scene: a living room.

(Scene takes place in a living room, with two men sitting on a couch and their daughter is on the floor.)

DAUGHTER
Daddy, where do babies come from?

DADDY 1
Mommies have babies dear, that's where they come from.

DAUGHTER
Do boys ever have babies?

DADDY 1
No dear, only mommies.

DAUGHTER
Megan says you have to have a mommy and a daddy to have a baby.

---

[36] Gradual report. "Where do Babies Come From?!?!?!?!" YouTube. 29 December 2009. Web. 3 July 2011.

DADDY 2

We should spend a little less time over at Megan's house.

DADDY 1

What Megan means is that it takes a man and a woman to make a baby, that's all.

DAUGHTER

She said that mommies and daddies have to get married first.

DADDY 1

No sweetheart, you don't have to marry to have a baby.

DAUGHTER

Then, what's marriage for?

VOICEOVER

Let's not confuse our kids. Protect marriage by protecting the real meaning of marriage, between a man and a woman, vote yes on Proposition 8.[37]

This video is less worried about how babies come into this world from a technical, biological stand point, and more worried about making the argument that babies should only come into the world via married heterosexual parents: "Then, what's marriage for?" The commercial is arguing against same sex marriage by making the following points: mommies give birth to babies; however, you need a mommy and a daddy to make babies. A daddy cannot have or make a baby on his own. Babies should only be made within the confines of marriage. So this family, a daughter with same sex parents, is wrong and unnatural because only a man and woman can make babies. The logic behind this rhetoric is poor and highly

---

[37] yesonprop81025. "Proposition 8 Commercial." 25 October 2008. YouTube. 3 July 2011.

bewildering. The commercial ends with this sentence: "let's not confuse our kids." What? Talk about confusing, we have an argument that heterosexual marriage is needed for baby creation. We know this is not true. Hell, babies are created under all sorts of social conditions, most of which do not concern marriage or even heterosexual marriage: in test tubes, using turkey basters and sperm banks, in the back seat of cars, because of sexual assault, just to name a few. If, however, what the commercial argues was true, then this young girl would not exist and this family, with two dads, could not exist! Yet somehow, even in a fictional world of YouTube, the family exists. Truly this family exists outside of the confines of imagination, in households throughout the world. The only sane and reasonably honest line in this commercial was: "No sweetheart, you don't have to marry to have a baby." The biological creation of a child has nothing to do with social and economic arrangements, and it is wrong to link procreation with marriage.

As a society, we argue that it is helpful to raise a child within the confines of a social contract, such as marriage, because it offers more support for each member of the social unit. But even social arrangements do not constitute families. Families are not defined through marriage and confusing a social convention with a biological process is like confusing pumpkin seeds with fetuses. Regarding families, Mom used to say: "families do not always grow up under the same roof." Sometimes they do but often they do not. A mother and a father are only a mother and a Father insofar as they nurture and care for their children – otherwise, they are willing or not willing sperm and egg donors. Giving birth to or making a child does not equate family; families are earned and the title of mommy or daddy is also earned, and must be earned over and over again. My mother's first memory in life was rape, and she was a very young child at the time. She was raped by one of her "step-fathers." Here was a heterosexual relationship, a man and a woman with a baby, but there was no family, no real marriage. When I think upon Mom's early life, I am often reminded of that great movie, *Parenthood* (1989), directed by Ron Howard and starring Steve Martin. In this film, Keanu Reeves' character, Tod Higgins, remarks: "You know, Mrs. Buckman, you need a license to buy a dog, to drive a car; hell, you even need a license to catch a fish. But they'll let any butt-reaming asshole be a father."[38] This line struck me, and everyone in my family, profoundly when we watched the movie together in our Seattle living room. It became one of Mom's favorite sayings, but she adjusted the quote to better resemble her situation: "you have to get a license to drive a car, but any asshole can make a kid." Mom had it hard in her beginning life with sex and sexuality, and she worked to make sure her children did not have it as hard as she did. Although a lover of historic mythology, she did not fill us with folklore about sex or sexuality, and thought it essential that we always knew the truth and had good information. She wanted to protect us from the myth of "family," of sex, of sexuality and birth control, as well as the myths she was given about menopause. When it came to the topic and reality of female sexuality, Mom felt betrayed her entire life. This is likely why she saw eyeballs everywhere. Truth be told, "Big Brother" is watching and working to control women's sexuality, not only in the Middle East, Ireland, India or places in Africa, as we are told on the nightly news, but in the West as well. Yep, in the United States of America. It is interesting to note, at least symbolically, that the shape of a pumpkin seed resembles that of an eyeball.

---

[38] JULIEeTOD. "Keanu Reeves in 'Parenthood.'" YouTube. 8 August 2008. Web. 28 August 2012.

Continuous Conversations: First Sexual Experience

I asked my friends: How old were you the first time you had sex? Did you use birth control? If so, what did you use and was it easy to use?

Single, fifteen and horny. I did not [use birth control]. It was before AIDS was a threat and I was between cycles. [I] Felt safe.
    --Daniella G.

16 and single. No protection used.
    --Christy W.

Single, out of High School. Sad to say, no I did not [use birth control].
    --KD

I was fourteen, and while that seems terribly, terribly young, I was the last girl in my circle of friends to have sex. The very first time I had sex I used the 'withdrawal' method. I was just damned lucky it worked.
    --Kelly W.

Oh lord, I was fourteen. That is young. I had been with the boy (16) for a year and he was (and still is) a nice fellow. No birth control the first time out. Not sure I even considered it.

--Amy G.

Fifteen. I didn't live in Kentucky so I was still single. No [birth control].

-- Frank N.C.

The Diaphragm Blues

I was born in July 1966, at the Tucson Medical Center in AZ. Margaret Sanger, the individual that led the campaign for birth control in the United States, died at Tucson Medical Center on September 6, 1966. She was 82 years old. Regarding her passing, the New York Times wrote:

> As the originator of the phrase "birth control" and its best-known advocate, Margaret Sanger survived federal indictments, a brief jail term, numerous lawsuits, hundreds of street-corner rallies and raids on her clinics to live to see much of the world accept her view that family planning is a basic human right. The dynamic, titian-haired woman whose Irish ancestry also endowed her with unfailing charm and persuasive wit was first and foremost a feminist. She sought to create equality between the sexes by freeing women from what she saw as sexual servitude.[39]

Margaret Sanger provides me great inspiration, and I find it comforting to imagine that at some moment our paths crossed. Who knows, Sanger might have been in for a check-up or a hospital visit the day I was born, and she may have

---

[39] N.A. "Margaret Sanger is Dead at 82; Led Campaign for Birth Control." *The New York Times.* 7 September 1966. Web. 7 July 2011.

grabbed my tiny little hand and smiled at me. Of course, this is unlikely since Sanger was declared senile in 1962, diagnosed with advanced arteriosclerosis, and had suffered years of pain from two heart attacks, not to mention an addiction to the painkiller Demerol.[40] Time and space are strange concepts, and it wasn't until many years later that I found out we shared the same space, Tucson, for a little over a month before she left this world. I am not entirely sure why I take comfort in this fact, but I am positive that the research I did as a young woman into the life of Margaret Sanger changed my life entirely, sending me back to graduate school, helping me finance my education and saddling me with the diaphragm. Reflecting on my early research on Sanger, what I learned was that before the ravages of time robbed her body and mind, she was an unstoppable woman who changed reality in the U.S., helping to free up the rights of women. Although contraception was practiced and used in many countries outside of the U.S., including Holland during Sanger's time, it was illegal in the U.S. – it was even illegal to talk about it, at least through the U.S. mail.

When it comes to an American audience, the diaphragm and all forms of birth control have been and continue to be a hard sell. Historically, along with the crusade to make alcohol consumption illegal, several of the same participants within the temperance movement worked to outlaw birth control devices, and all information regarding contraception. This occurred at the start of the nineteenth century, and by 1873 congress passed the Comstock Act, popularly known as the Comstock Laws, which effectively outlawed the dissemination of information about birth control, women's sexuality, sexual infections and diseases (STD), including STD transmission and cures, through the mail, and other informational outlets. Thus in a free country information became illegal, and the

---

[40] Arteriosclerosis is a heart disease where the walls of the arteries start to thicken and harden.

topics of birth control, sexuality transmitted diseases, women's sexuality, and the female reproductive system were understood as obscene. This might explain why "Dick" is an accepted term for the male sexual organ as well as a proper first name, but the word "vagina" is still thought of as an obscene term, too horrible to say in public, as Lisa Brown, State representative for Michigan, district 39, found out.[41] Regardless, the Comstock law was named after Anthony Comstock, the head of the New York Society for the Suppression of Vice (NYSSV), in 1872. With the help of very wealthy donors, Comstock was able to lobby the New York State Legislature to criminalize premarital sex, adultery, as well as the use and discussion of birth control. This Comstock Law also had the so-called added benefit of making divorce and staying single more difficult. Remembering her tangle with these laws, Margaret Sanger recounted one of the many battles that she had with Anthony Comstock regarding an article of hers that included the words gonorrhea and syphilis:

> The words gonorrhea and syphilis had occurred in that article and Anthony Comstock, headed the New York Society for the Suppression of Vice, did not like them. By this so called, Comstock Law of 1873, which had been adroitly pushed through a busy Congress on the eve of adjournment, the Post Office had been given authority to decide what might be called lewd, lascivious, indecent, or obscene, and this extraordinary man had been granted the extraordinary power, alone of all citizens of the United States, to open any letter or package or pamphlet or book passing through the mail and, if you wish, lay his complaint before the post office.[42]

---

[41] Brown, Lisa. "Lisa Brown: Silenced for saying (shock!) 'Vagina'" *CNN Opinion*. 21 June 2012. Web. 19 September 2012.

[42] Sanger, Margaret. *An Autobiography*. New York, N. Y: Dover Publishers, 2004. Pp. 77-78. Print.

Sadly, the medical community, especially doctors, often sided with Comstock, refusing to offer information regarding sexuality and birth control to women. If you were a man, on the other hand, and you were thinking of visiting "a house of ill repute," then care for sexually transmitted diseases (STDs), information, and condoms were readily available and supplied. Why this gender discrimination? Many doctors felt women would end up rejecting their expected roles within marriage. After all, some of the most important wifely duties were to have sex and produce children (preferably male heirs) for one's husband. During the nineteenth century it was not uncommon for women to have seven or more children inside of marriage and, as Margaret Sanger demonstrated, the poorer the class system a woman came from, the more likely she had more children than she could afford to care for. In today's world, Sanger is often criticized for working in the poorer areas of New York, rather than in "rich" areas. She is also criticized for her adopting the then popular idea of eugenics, a theory she rejected.[43] Sanger never called for the "genocide" of blacks, poor people, other minorities or women. She did

---

[43] The Theory of eugenics was originally supported by many of Sanger's contemporaries, including: Winston Churchill, Marie Stopes, H.G. Wells, Theodore Roosevelt, George Bernard Shaw, John Maynard Keynes, John Harvey Kellogg, Linus Pauling and Sidney Webb, to name just a few. However, like Sanger, as the theory was applied toward the injustice of racism and genderism, it was abandoned by many of these historic figures. See: Wikipedia contributors. "Eugenics." *Wikipedia, The Free Encyclopedia*. 9 August 2012. Web. 10 August 2012. It should also be remember that in 1927, the Supreme Court upheld a decision to allow Virginia to sterilize women consider mentally challenged (See Buck VS Bell, decision written by high justice Oliver Wendell Holmes, Jr.). As such, a legal form of eugenics functioned in the U.S. as well. It is nice to know that humans continue to rise above bad theories and learn from their mistakes.

call for an end of giving birth to unwanted children, abandoned and discarded on the streets or in state run institutions all because of a lack of birth control and education. And who had the least amount of medical help and education? Those in poorer socio-economic classes. Yet instead of examining the full historical account of the rise of Planned Parenthood, critics such as Herman Cain and others do not bother to research the full facts, but reconstruct history so it suits alternative, often religious motives. Consider for a moment, this interview between Herman Cain and Bob Schieffer during an episode of *Face the Nation;* the transcript was later posted on *The Washington Post:*

Bob Schieffer

OK. I want to ask you, since we're on the subject of abortion, there was, at one point back there when the question of Planned Parenthood came up, and you said that it was not Planned Parenthood, it was really planned genocide because you said Planned Parenthood was trying to put all these centers into the black communities because they wanted to kill black babies –

Herman Cain

Yes.

Schieffer

-- before they were born. Do you still stand by that?

Cain

I still stand by that.

Schieffer

Do you have any proof that that was the objective of Planned Parenthood?

Cain

If people go back and look at the history and look at
Margaret Sanger's own words, that's exactly where that
came from. Look up the history. So if you go back and
look up the history -- secondly, look at where most of
them were built; 75 percent of those facilities were built in
the black community -- and Margaret Sanger's own words,
she didn't use the word "genocide," but she did talk about
preventing the increasing number of poor blacks in this
country by preventing black babies from being born.[44]

The problem is simple: Cain did not research the history of
Margaret Sanger or Planned Parenthood because if he had, he
would have discovered that the largest number of childhood
mortality, mother mortality, for self-induced abortions and
complications from child birth, and the highest number of
births during Sanger's time occurred in areas of high poverty.
Further, Sanger did not promote abortion but focused on
birth control. Since the black community was extremely
discriminated against in the early 1920s, many blacks lived in
the poorest of neighborhoods. But Sanger also opened her
clinics in poverty driven Jewish neighborhoods and other areas
as well. The common denominator in this equation? Poverty.
Not the color of one's skin or the practice of one's religion ....
poverty. Yet those who equate birth control with abortion
tend to also equate Planned Parenthood with genocide, and
Margaret Sanger as genocide's inventor. But the logic does not
hold. Indeed, Sanger wanted to prevent the then sad reality of
death. She was tired of witnessing premature death, children
and mothers dying because of a vicious cycle where too many
children, no money, and no medical care equaled death every

---

[44] Kessler, Glenn. "Herman Cain's Rewriting of Birth-Control
History." *The Washington Post.* 1 November 2011. Web. 10 August
2012.

day. Consider the first ad for her clinic in Brooklyn, NY, which was located in a predominantly Jewish neighborhood: "Mothers! Can you afford to have a large family? Do you want anymore children? If not, why do you have them? DO NOT KILL, DO NOT TAKE LIFE, BUT prevent. Safe, harmless information can be obtained by trained nurses at 46 Amboy Street, Near Pitkin Ave. – Brooklyn" (emphasis in original).[45] Sanger chose this location, and all additional locations for her clinics, using a number of criteria, many of which focused on the problem of poverty in relation to medical care and access to care. As Cain requested, let's continue to examine Sanger's words specifically. Writing in her *Autobiography*, Sanger wrote:

> The selection of a suitable locality was of the greatest importance. I tramped through the streets of the Bronx, Brooklyn, the lower sides of Manhattan, East and West. I scrutinize the Board of Health vital statistics of all the boroughs – births and infant and maternal mortality in relation to low wages, and also the number of philanthropic institutions in the vicinity.[46]

Today's critics are less concerned with actual history and more concerned with making a misguiding argument in order to promote specific religious ideologies. These agendas argue against women having control over their bodies, especially when it comes to the issue of birth control and also, abortion. For those who wish to destroy Planned parenthood, their attack approach and corresponding rhetoric is clear: *If we demonize Margaret Sanger, making her a scapegoat, we can then weaken*

---

[45] Sanger, Margaret. "Sanger's First Clinic." *Margaret Sanger Paper Project Research Annex.* Jill Grimaldi, ed. 26 October 2010. Web. 19 August 2012.

[46] Sanger, Margaret. *Margaret Sanger: An Autobiography.* Whitefish, MT: Kessinger Pub, 2004. P. 213. Print. It is interesting to note that the women of the neighborhood invited Sanger to open her first clinic there.

Planned Parenthood's ability to have access to public funds for women's health care. But make no mistake; this smear campaign is far less about genocide, and more about a socio-political agenda, and the effort to outlaw birth control and abortion. The fear is not about what happens to children after they are born; rather, the concern is centered on sperm-egg collisions. Talk about the Diaphragm Blues.

The debate offered by Cain, and those who take his line of argument, is no different from the debate that existed during Margaret Sanger's time. What constitutes death? Getting pregnant and then having your child die? Or preventing pregnancy? When I think on those past days, as well as our modern sensibility that promotes the political and "religious" arguments against birth control, I cannot help but think of that mighty funny song "Every Sperm is Sacred," by Monty Python.[47]

Here is a critical argument for you! In this comic routine, from the movie *The Meaning Of Life*, the audience is presented with two extreme depictions of religious families: one Catholic and one Protestant. The Catholic family is experiencing a difficult situation where the father and mother must sell all their children, because they can no longer afford to feed them. As this song argues, according to Catholics, birth control is against God's will because every sperm is sacred. Waste not, want not, as they say. We understand from the girth of this onscreen family, avoiding sex is also not an option for the good Catholic! The obvious solution? Have lots of sex, have lots of kids, and sell the kids for food so that you can have more sex, more kids, and more kiddo yard sales: *Don't miss this week's two for one blue-light special!* In the next scene, we are shown the absurd opposite end of the spectrum with a childless Protestant couple. Under Protestantism, birth control

---

[47] Howman, David, Andre Jaquemin, Terry Joes, and Michael Palin. "Every Sperm is Sacred." *Monty Python's The Meaning of Life.* Universal Pictures, 1983. Film.

is allowed, but apparently the Protestant never bothers to practice sex because that would be ... sticky? Oh the irony. I can't help but think that Margaret Sanger would have loved this song. Regardless, it is important to note that Sanger was never against children being born, or even against one's wish for a large family, but she wanted to give women the ability to make a choice. Families should be planned; families should not be accidental, and all children should be wanted. After all, sometimes "God" does give us more then we can handle; for example, a world with strained resources where famine exists, a world where unclean water exists, a world where rape exists, and a world where too many children in an economically challenged household can lead to child and spouse abuse and/or abandonment. It happens all the time. The decision to bring a child into this world is far too important to be left up to chance.

Dismissing chance for action, on November 10, 1921, Margaret Sanger formed the *American Birth Control League* to provide education, establish legal reforms, and offer research regarding family planning. This organization grew out of a publication, *The Birth Control Review*, which started in 1917.[48] The very first issue of *The Birth Control Review* asked an important ethical question regarding the Comstock laws: *Shall We Break This Law?* Applying the philosophy of utilitarianism, Margaret Sanger argued in her first review that some laws must be broken simply because they are unethical and do not serve the greater good: "No law is too sacred to break," wrote Margaret Sanger who also provided a history of law-breakers fighting for ethical outcomes:

> Throughout all the ages, the beacon lights of human progress have been lit by the law-breaker. Moses, the deliverer, was a law-breaker. Christ, the carpenter, was a

---

[48] *The Birth Control Review* had a very long run, and was published through January of 1940.

law-breaker and his early followers practiced [sic] their religion in defiance of the law of that time. Joan of Arc was a law-breaker. So, too, were George Washington and the heroes of the American Revolution.[49]

A wise and critical thinker, Margaret Sanger used the same array of Biblical references, Christian heroes, and American patriotism being waved by those who supported the erroneous Comstock Law. She was adamant that this law was un-American, since it stood in stark opposition to the American values of liberty, freedom, and the pursuit of happiness.

Besides her fight against the Comstock law, Margaret Sanger is also responsible for opening the first birth control clinic in the United States, in 1916, Brooklyn, New York. Hundreds of women attended this clinic, but within a month the clinic was closed, Sanger, her sister, and fellow supporters were all arrested. While the clinic was open, and this is where her story affects my story, women were fitted with diaphragms, one of the most effective methods of birth control, and a method Margaret Sanger learned about studying in Holland and France: "In 1883 Dr. Mensinga a gynecologist of Flensburg, Germany, had published a description of a contraceptive device called a diaphragm pessary, which he and Dr. Jacobs had perfected. Dr. and Madame Hoitsema Rutgers had taken charge of the League in 1899 and with such success that the work had spread through that well-ordered kingdom."[50] After many legal battles, Margaret Sanger's clinics finally grew and these clinics were eventually known as *The Planned Parenthood Federation of America,* first established in 1946. Sanger and Planned Parenthood preferred the diaphragm,

---

[49] Sanger, Margaret. "Shall We Break This Law." *The Birth Control Review*. 1:1, February 1917.
[50] Sanger, Margaret. *Margaret Sanger: An Autobiography*. Whitefish, MT: Kessinger Pub, 2004. P. 143. Print.

promoting it as the safest and most effective means of birth control.

I think the words "slippery when wet" should be included with the instructions offered for the use and implementation of this contraceptive device. This should be said and recognized upfront, as an introductory preface to this particular form of birth control. As I have noted earlier, Mom was very frank when it came to the issues of sex, sexuality, and birth control. She came from a generation where women had babies early, often unplanned and unwanted. Indeed, she was one of those children. By the time I was entering my adolescence, the U.S. was experiencing a bubble in child pregnancy and Nancy Reagan's rhetoric against drug use and early sexual engagement, "just say no," was about to become a great failure. Mom didn't want me to be a statistic. She wanted me to be prepared should I decide to have sex. She did not want me to make the decision regarding having sex lightly; birth control was not designed for an easy out. Rather, Mom wanted me equipped to handle my own sex life. After all, we would not send a soldier to war without training in the use of weapons. We do not send surgeons into surgery without first training them in the art of the scalpel, ergo we should not allow people to enter sexual relations without proper training about sex, sexuality, STD, and birth control. So it was in my freshman year of high school that my family went on a field trip to Planned Parenthood, where I was to get some education regarding sex, sexuality, and my very first female check-up. I was also going to obtain birth control ... because ... you know ... just in case. Like Margaret Sanger, Mom did not have a great deal of faith that a young man would be prepared and ready with proper birth control should that fateful day come about.

You, dear reader, might have already clued in to the *Twilight Zone* moment of this particular life event: my first female exam and procurement of birth control was part of a *family field trip* that started out at Planned Parenthood, ended at the local

Dairy Queen, and was topped off with a banana split food fight. Talk about fun! Seriously, how many families make this type of thing an all inclusive field trip including parents, siblings, and the person waiting to be put under the microscope of female hell: a gynecological exam? As you might have guessed, such an event was not off the beaten path for my family. We celebrated all life's landmark events: Birthdays, weddings, coming of age, even events involving strange round plastic diaphragm thingies. My years of experience using the slip-n-slide should account for something, after all.

I'll never forget when I got my period ... oh hell on earth! I say this with a combination of horror, delight, and just a little bit more horror thrown in for good measure. Why? Simply because when you are a thirteen year-old girl, having your period for the first time, even if you're prepared for it, is a frightening experience. Growing up, ack! Honestly, the first time I noticed hair under my arms, it was enough to send me to my bedroom for three months. I really did not want to grow up, since I had no interest in becoming a "woman." I enjoyed being a child, and I enjoyed being a tomboy even more, so these signs of impending womanhood were offensive, threatening, and unwelcome. When I got my period for the first time, Mom was overjoyed. She sent Lee-Dad[51] to the market for menstrual pads because she only used tampons, and Mom didn't think I would like to use them the first time out. However, a family friend was at the house, and she tried to teach me how to use a tampon. Oh my God. Let me just say that again ... Oh my God! Talk about an epic failure, not only was it a tampon, but it was one of those tampons without an applicator. Again, hell for a thirteen year old. Lee-Dad, savior at that moment, came home from the store with pads,

---

[51] I am blessed with two fathers. To avoid "Dad" confusion, I call my step dad "Lee-Dad" and my biological father "Fred-Dad."

beaming, announcing to the world, it seemed, that I was now a woman:

"Mom, you don't think he told that to the guy at Seven-Eleven, do you?" Oh yes, he did:

My Girl's a Woman Now

Scene: a 7-ll store, somewhere in Tucson, AZ.

(A proud father walks up to the checkout with a box of menstrual pads in hand, and it's "a proud day in my life" look shining from his face.)

LEE-DAD
Good day sir, I would like to buy these menstrual pads.

STORE CLERK
Why certainly good man. I'm assuming they're not for you?

BOTH
(Laughs.)

LEE-DAD
No indeed not, but I hear they make good odor-eaters for your shoes.[52]

BOTH
(The two men laugh again.)

---

[52] I wish I could say that this line was a figment of my ample imagination; however, this was actually said to my husband the first time he purchased supplies for me, where the 7-11 clerk offered to throw in a "bonus" Winston's cigarette hat - we are still not sure why or what the bonus hat had to do with menstrual pads. Awkward....

LEE-DAD

No, they're for my daughter; she is a woman today.

STORE CLERK

Well, congratulations. I guess you're going to be locking her up from now on, right?

(Both men chuckle.)

LEE-DAD

Yep! The next stop is the local armory. Yes indeed, I'm buying the best chastity belt money can purchase!

STORE CLERK

Good luck with that! You are a wise man sir, a wise man.

BOTH

(Both men laugh.)

(Scene fades to black.)

To be fair, Lee-Dad did not buy me a chastity belt; but to also be honest, he did threaten to buy one several times as a sort of a preemptive strike against the loss of my virginity. Regardless, Lee-Dad came home with pads, a cake, and a six-pack of Coca-Cola. Afterwards, phone calls were made spreading the "joyous" news, and an impromptu "she is a woman now" party was thrown. After the party, I ran to my bedroom and attempted to stay there for a good year and a half, coming out only for food, school, and a John Denver concert.

I wish I could say this last part was a joke or even an exaggeration, but it was not. I did not want to become a woman; I did not want to grow up. It really was not so much that I was embarrassed about my family's excitement for me, or the celebration, or even the candid nature my family's approach to the topics of sex, sexuality, and growing up. I just did not want to grow up. I understood the consequences very well and I did not, still do not, like them. I liked baseball. I liked running. I liked building huts out in the desert. I loved acting and roller-skating. I liked hanging out with boys, and I didn't want boys to start seeing me as something different. But whether we wish to grow up or not, it happens. Despite my refusal, by freshman year in high school I was boy crazy. Recently I came across a journal I kept back then, and I laughed at the deep longing found in each line of text. Each year I had a new crush on a different young man. Oh the panging! Oh the melodramatic confessions of a teenager in "heavy like." One entry read: "Dear God, if you are there and you can hear me, then please make _____ ask me out. He is so beautiful and a football player, and I know I could just love him forever. I know I said that about _____, but this time it's really true!!!!!! Please God do this one thing for me." I was better off as a tomboy.

Besides my boy craziness, I was a teenager with all those teenager chemical reactions going on in my body. After my freshman year, my family moved to Seattle and I started to hang out with the drama crowd. On Friday nights, sophomore through junior year of high school, friends and I attended and became cast members for the local showing of *The Rocky Horror Picture Show* at the historic Neptune Theatre in the University District, Seattle. Like you might find on current roller derby women today, we dressed in corsets, ripped fishnet stockings, high-heel shoes, and sang musical-rock songs about sex and sexuality.[53] No wonder Mom wanted me to go to Planned Parenthood, and no wonder she wanted me prepared. But that first visit to Planned Parenthood was even more awkward and surreal than when I got my period.

---

[53] O'Brien, Richard. "Touch-a, Touch-a, Touch-a, Touch Me." *The Rocky Horror Show: Musical*. New York: French, 1983. Print.

The Diaphragm Fitting

Scene: a Planned Parenthood clinic.

(Lighting and style of scene resembles a type of surreal nightmare, in the guise of a black and white "private dick" dime-store novel. Lights come up on a corridor of a Planned Parenthood Clinic. The main character, Becky, walks into an examination room that has an oversize "B" hanging over the door.)

BECKY
(Unless otherwise indicated, dialogue is voiced over the action, while our subject seems to mostly suffer silently through the events. All movements are very crisp and highly stylized.)

Alone, I walk down a short hall and into the first examination room on the right. Examination room 'B.' 'B' for birth control. The room is white. Sterile ... as an examination room should be. There is a gown laid out for me, but I don't know any better ... I think it's a smock. There are all types of gadgets here. Gloves. Steel duck-beak looking clamps. Magazines. Jelly in tubes. A poster hangs on the ceiling. It's a butterfly. It reminds me of my grandmother's butterfly collection. The butterfly represents a woman's genitalia. I think about my grandmother's collection. Dead butterflies under thick plastic. The moment is timeless, hanging over my head like the butterfly poster. Then ... she comes in, the Doctor.

(A pair of sexy, long legs in dark stockings and high-heeled shoes enters the scene. We never see the doctor's body or face, only her legs. The legs should "act" out the dialogue.)

She has the kind of legs that straight men or gay women would die for: Long, slinky and smooth. The legs interrogate me with questions:

DR. LEGS
(Shooting out her questions like she was an auctioneer.)

Are you sexually active? Do you experience frequent yeast infections? When was your last menstruation? Would you happen to have a mint? I had hummus for lunch, you know.

(Legs sit and cross her legs, in a purposeful fashion.)

BECKY
(Focus on Becky's legs and fingers, nervously playing with her shirt. Compared to Dr. Legs, Becky's legs are short and hairy, a little too much hair for comfort.)

I answer all her questions. Calm. Cool. Steady as a jackhammer. Dr. Legs tells me about birth control. She describes my options the way Mick Jagger sings rock-n-roll. Rough and tempting.

DR. LEGS
Now remember, not all birth control protects against STDs. Regardless, there are over the counter options: rubbers, sponges, and such. Of course, there is the birth control pill; some prescriptions will even clean up that acne you are sporting, dear. The IUD is now well received and the diaphragm is a classic, a classic dear. Indeed, the diaphragm is a low cost and a highly effective choice. Margaret Sanger championed the diaphragm, you know!

BECKY
I agree, and so the diaphragm is my choice of armor. Dr. Legs puts on rubber gloves, and then tells me to lie down on the

examination table. I assume the position for my first female exam. You know the kind, take your clothes off, put on the "gown," put your feet into the cold steel hand shaped stirrups that open you up like the Ballard Locks (creaking sound).[54] The medieval steel speculum looks like a duck's beak ... quack. Dr. Legs inserts the beak into my vagina and spreads me as wide as possible; I had no idea how flexible I could be.

DR. LEGS

Now, press down like you're going to have a bowel movement, but of course, don't dear.

BECKY

Legs is no quack. Everything is fine. What a relief. I'm then measured for the correct diaphragm size; by the look of it, I get the baby-model. I'm shown how to insert the diaphragm.

DR. LEGS

First you take the sperm jelly and place a small amount, like a teaspoon, in the cup of the diaphragm. Then you take your finger and rub the substance onto the outer rim. There! Now you bend the diaphragm into the shape of a taco and insert it into the vagina, all, all, all the way up. If you will notice, one difference between a taco and the diaphragm is that you eat one, and insert the other. Ha, Ha ... I sternly suggest that you are careful not to confuse the two opposing functions. The result could be disastrous!

BECKY

After this informative lecture, Legs leaves me alone to practice—throwing me away like a used Kleenex. I'm clear on

---

[54] Really, any "locks" that control the flow of water will do. I live in Seattle and so what comes to mind are the Ballard Locks. Feel free to insert any "locks" you may know for your personal comfort and familiarity.

my assignment: Get the diaphragm in. Take the diaphragm out. Simple enough. But this assignment is filled with gels and rubber; I've never been very good with the slippery and the stretchy; pantyhose still elude me. First, I put the spermicide into the cup of the diaphragm and around the edges. Now, I fold the diaphragm into the shape of a taco. The gesture makes me hungry. After it's folded, I ease it into my vagina and hope I don't have to go fishing. No fear of losing it; I can't get it in. I wonder, do boys think of this on their first time out; their first time in? Out. In. Out. In. But I digress. The diaphragm flies across the floor and lands on dust bunnies. I go through a tube of spermicide. Will this farce never end? I decide to give it one more try, if not for me, for Dr. Legs. I remember one fateful summer in little league. The last inning. Reds ahead by one. It's up to me to bring in the winning runs. The bases are loaded. My hands slide around the bat with a tight grip and then the swing. The diaphragm goes flying through the air and attaches itself to the ceiling. The game is lost. Dr. Legs comes in with a broom and knocks it loose.

DR. LEGS
No worries dear, it happens to the best of us, you know.

BECKY
Dr. Legs sends me home. I'm not in her league. On the way out she looks at me the way Babe Ruth looks at a fan and tells me ...

DR. LEGS
If at first you don't succeed, try, try again. If you still don't get the hang of it, there is always the pill my dear.

(Legs tap her way out of the examination room.)

BECKY
Yes, there is always the pill.

69

(Lights fade to black as we see Becky looking apprehensively at her new diaphragm.)

I am suspicious that the diaphragm scene from the 1984 movie *The Hotel New Hampshire* was inspired by similar true-life events. If you have not seen this movie, do; you must at least see it for the diaphragm scene, if for nothing else. In case there is not a universal recall of this bit of film nostalgia, here's quick overview. One of the main characters, John, takes a beautiful rich girl, Bitty Tuck, nicknamed "Titsie" for her, you guessed it, large breasts, to his family's New Years Eve Party in their new hotel. John and Bitty get ready to have a quickie in an upstairs room when poor Bitty's diaphragm gets lost, while she faints after seeing the family's dead, now taxidermied, dog named Shadow lying in a tub full of water. John's sister declares: "fainted while diaphragming." To be fair, there were no dead taxidermy dogs around, and I did not faint while learning how to insert the diaphragm, but I came close to it when I heard Lee-Dad speak loudly from the waiting room: "why is she going in my daughter's room with a broom?" My family is not big with "thinking things in our head" etiquette; rather, we are blurters. I remember during my college years at Cornish College of the Arts when I played the lead in *Not By Bed Alone*, a French farce by Georges Feydea. In this show, I had to enhance my chest to offer the illusion that I had "Titsie" ample breasts. Unlike "Titsie" in the *Hotel New Hampshire*, I am not well endowed, and so the effect was created with a push-up bra, as well as heavy shadowing and shading make-up work. As I entered the stage one performance, I heard Mom blurt out, "Oh my God, my daughter has boobs!" I mean this sincerely: I love my mom and miss her daily.

Refocusing off of breasts, or lack of breasts, and back to the topic of diaphragms and the diaphragm blues, remember that warning offered a few pages back? Slippery when wet?

Diaphragms are just that. I am not sure about wet taxidermied dogs, but that is for someone else to discover, I hope. After many failed attempts to get the diaphragm into my body and in the correct position, my last attempt at this mission had the diaphragm flying out of my fingers and making a suction hold onto the ceiling. Don't ask me how. I do not know how, or why, or even the science of it all, but may I say again: Oh my God! The diaphragm stuck to the ceiling briefly, and then it rather unstuck, slid down a wall and fell behind a large medical cabinet. I put my cloths back on, tossed the so-called gown, and called in the nurse who came in with a broom in order to "fish" the diaphragm out from under the cabinet. All the while my father's words echoed throughout the clinic: "why is she going in my daughter's room with a broom?" I was sent home to practice on my own with a new diaphragm and a new tube of spermicide. I did not lose my virginity for many years, likely in fear of having to put that damn thing in to me. After I was released, we all went to Dairy Queen for banana splits. Mom and I got into an ice cream fight, and that was that. My diaphragm sat unused for years, but I was armed and ready, at least, in that department.

I've had a love/hate relationship with the diaphragm my entire life, because of one crazy occurrence after another with this round, spaceship looking rubber barrier. However, even with all the mishaps that have occurred with the diaphragm, I have never gotten pregnant while using it, and that says a great deal about its effectiveness. Indeed, the diaphragm is said to be so effective that when used correctly, only six out of one hundred women will get pregnant.[55] I am grateful to Margaret Sanger and Planned Parenthood for helping me have a choice in the matter of having children. Families should be planned for. As an adult, I decided not to have children, but this decision was based upon many factors, and each factor weighed out heavily and seriously. It is not that I did not want

---

[55] NA. "Diaphragm." *Planned Parenthood.* ND. Web. 13 July 2011.

children; rather, it is simply that I wanted to be sure, or at least somewhat sure, that I could care for any child I brought into this world. I could not make that claim during my "childbearing" years. Regardless, I have used Planned Parenthood throughout my life not only as a place to get access to affordable birth control, but for my general medical needs as well, especially during those times when I was without access to Health Care. I have gotten yearly health checkups with this organization, blood workups, and HIV / STD testing and screening. Furthermore, Planned Parenthood helped me earn my higher education through a community service project for a fellowship I was awarded. While working with them, I was educated as an HIV councilor, and I had an opportunity to create and start a safe sex program, handing out safe sex packets to nightclubs around Orlando, FL. I also wrote and performed a play for the Orlando International Fringe Festival, as a benefit for the Orlando Planned Parenthood clinic. I did not raise all that much money for the clinic, but I cannot tell you how proud I was to be of help.

Today, as it has been true for most of Planned Parenthood's history, birth control and clinics are under fire and several states, including New Hampshire, oddly enough, are pulling public funds from Planned Parenthood because these clinics offer abortions. Somehow people have the mistaken belief that abortions are all these clinics do, as organizations such as the *Susan G. Komen for the Cure*,[56] as well as states, and individuals conveniently forget that as a medical clinic, Planned Parenthood offers many services including general health services, cancer screening, birth control, as well as HIV/STD screening and counseling. In New Hampshire, many people, men and women, will be without access to birth control, antibiotic treatment for urinary tract infections, medication for STDs, as well as other services because of a

---

[56] Makovsky, Ken. "Lessons Learned: the Komen-Parenthood Affair." *Forbs.com*. 13 February 2012. Web. 13 February 2012.

loss in state support. Since most states are cutting their own health care programs as a result of widespread budget cuts occurring throughout the U.S., hundreds of men and woman will have nowhere to turn: "We have to send them away with a prescription knowing that without insurance, they have to pay the full cost of that at a local pharmacy, and many patients have told us they're not gonna have the money in their budget to afford to fill those prescriptions."[57] I am saddened to see the life's work of Margaret Sanger chipped away and discarded. But I am even sadder to see that as a nation, regarding a woman's reproductive rights, we would rather embrace Comstock, denying women and men the right to decide when to have a family, and how many children to have. I am glad that Margaret Sanger is not here to see the lack of progress made today. Sadly, I have learned in this life that the ethics, social views, and laws around the American values of freedom, liberty, and the pursuit of happiness are a lot like the Diaphragm Blues in the end: slippery when wet.

---

[57] Bassett, Laura. "Planned Parenthood Defunded in New Hampshire." *The Huffington Post.* 11 July 2011. Web. 13 July 2011.

Continuous Conversations: Sexual Assault

I asked my friends: Where you ever raped or sexually assaulted? If so, at what age and did you know your attacker?

Sexually assaulted by my uncle at 14. I thought at the time I was a first class seductress. It wasn't till I was older that I understood it as assault.
--Daniella G.

I have never been raped or sexually assaulted. I know I am lucky in that sense.
- Jolie C.P.

Yes, twice. At 14 in a church parking lot. Again at 18 yrs by a business colleague of the family business.
--Christy A.W.

I believe I was 'fingered' while drinking down at the Space Needle, would have been 8th grade? Didn't know him.
--KD

My violin teacher in grade school used to make me play violin while he rubbed up against me. All the girls, not just me. I was nine. That was pretty gross. Also, once when I was 19, and out of my mind on drugs (having unknowingly smoked pot laced with pcp), my 'boyfriend' had sex with me. My memory told me that I had said no, but he told me I never spoke. I never knew for sure what the truth was until years later I found out he'd done that to another girl.

--Kelly W.

Yes, when I was 16 I did not know my attacker.

--Rachel M.

[I was] never raped THANK GOD! I have dealt with too many assaults at 6, 13, twice when I was 14, and 19. I knew all but two of them.

--Amber

Yes, I was probably 10 or 11 years old. The person was my best friend's step dad.

-Ilene M.

Would a Slut by Any Other Name Still Wear Stilettos?

On Father's Day, 2011, I was sitting in the middle of Westlake Center Square in Seattle waiting for the SlutWalk protest and march to arrive at my location. Having missed the actual march to the downtown area, I decided to show up for the larger protest that was to start at 12:30 PM. It was cold, very cold and windy, and although we were all encouraged to wear sexy, "slut" affirming outfits to the event, I dressed in jeans and layers. The protest was against society blaming the victim for his or her rape / sexual assault rather than holding the rapist responsible. One main point of contention held by the participants was that the clothing a person wears does not equal an invitation for sex, consensual or otherwise. It is frustrating how people often relate clothing to social cues: If you are a gay man, you dress like Barbara Streisand; if you are a businessman worth your weight in gold, you dress in an Italian hand-made suit; if you are a businesswoman, you dress like a businessman, so you can trick your fellow businessmen into thinking you are actually a man and not a woman! Clever, yes? If you are a slut or a roller derby skater, you show your underwear to the world as an open invitation for sex - right? Wrong. Our culture has a strange relationship to underclothing - an obsession, really, that starts in childhood. One of my favorite jokes when I was a child was this:

BECKY
Hey, wow, check that out. What's under there???

UNSUSPECTING TARGET
Under where?

BECKY
Ha, ha I made you say underwear!

Children are great when it comes to their nakedness and sexuality because they don't have assumed attitudes regarding sex yet. My nephew, like myself when I was his age, will occasionally run around the house naked, laughing and being silly. He has no concept of nakedness being wrong, yet he does know it's not okay to go outside naked. Innocence allows him to be himself. Unfortunately, children learn quickly to place value judgments not only on their nakedness and their body, but also on clothing. The underwear joke, for example, only becomes funny to children at the point when they start to associate the term "underwear" as being a forbidden, naughty word - a somehow questionable or offensive word. Underwear. Under wear, Underwear. A word that becomes taboo and tempting in a mysterious way. This is what SlutWalk confronts - the absurdity behind underwear as a type of forbidden/dangerous thing that tempts men into raping women.

The first SlutWalk occurred in April 2011, Toronto, Canada, incited by the words Constable Michael Sanguinetti uttered during a talk on crime prevention at York University, Osgoode: "women should avoid dressing like sluts" if they wish to avoid being victimized.[58] Although Const. Sanguinetti later apologized for his comment, these words, this moral, this

---

[58] Rush, Curtis. "Cop apologizes for 'sluts' remark at law school." *The Star*. 18 February 2011. Web. 20 June 2011.

rhetorical message struck a nerve with not only the original organizers of the event, Sonya Barnett and Heather Jarvis, but also with a cross section of people from all sexual orientations and genders around the world. Since that first walk in April of 2011, SlutWalks have occurred throughout the United States, notably in Chicago and Seattle; but also in other countries, including: Scotland, Glasgow and Edinburgh; São Paulo, Brazil; Amsterdam, Netherlands; Copenhagen, Denmark; England, London and Birmingham; Sydney, Australia; Brazil, Brasilia and Belo Horizonte; as well as Riyadh, Saudi Arabia.[59]

The movement is christened "SlutWalk" because many protesters wish to recapture the word *slut*, reforming the term for positive use. The issue comes down to language, socialization, and the deemed ethics that stem from this combination of forces. For those marginalized as "sluts" because of gender, fashion choice, or sexual preferences, there is a serious realization that a word can do more than hurt a human being's feelings, rather the label can victimize a person, leaving him or her open to guilt by label. As William Ryan wrote back in the early 1970s, attempts to blame a victim for his or her circumstance allows society to ask: "What's wrong with the victim" rather than "what's wrong with the attacker"?[60] The process of victim blaming creates marginalization and inequality.[61] It is a rhetorical way to justify an immoral act or crime as "the norm," the "way we do things here," rather than encouraging an active mode of questioning, challenging "the way things are done." Although Ryan was mostly concerned about addressing issues of poverty and racism in his pivotal text, *Blaming the Victim*, certainly we can

---

[59] Wikipedia contributors. "SlutWalk." *Wikipedia, The Free Encyclopedia.* 20 June 2011. Web. 20 June 2011.
[60] Ryan, William. *Blaming the Victim*. Revised and Updated. New York, NY: Vintage Books, 1976. P. 102. Kindle Edition.
[61] "Victim blaming" is a phrase coined by William Ryan and used by the SlutWalk community.

see a correlation alongside the application of the word "slut" with respect to rape and sexual assault victims.

"S/he was asking for it, did you see the way s/he dressed?"

"Oh yeah, that piece was smoking! S/he had it all hanging out for the taking."

On the SlutWalk Seattle website, organizers discuss the controversial move of adopting the word slut for the protests, explaining how there is a need to reclaim this word, making it a positive term "for a person of any gender who has and enjoys frequent sex, especially with multiple partners… Reappropriating "slut" serves three primary functions":

♦ Takes away the word's power to do harm as a pejorative - one of the best ways to fight hate is to embrace and disarm the words employed by the haters.

♦ Provides a sex-positive term for women, few of which exist (like "stud" is for men).

♦ Allow sluts to identify as part of a cohesive group for political representation (see identity politics).

As with any reappropriated/reclaimed word, you should NEVER use "slut" without explicit permission from the subject first, and that permission can be revoked at any time based on their discretion. The double standard that men are often praised for having lots of sex while women are shamed for it is an example of slut shaming.[62]

Although I find the movement's need to reclaim the ethos of slut important, my personal focus and concern is in the realm of legal and public victim blaming via "slut shaming." I was at SlutWalk because I wanted to be with other women

---

[62] NA. "FAQs and Examples of Victim Blaming and Slut Shaming." *SlutWalk Seattle*. 10 June 2011. Web. 14 July 2011.

who had been raped and blamed for that rape because of the clothing worn, or not worn. I wanted to stand up with the group publicly and say: "No More!" I wanted to do this for myself and for my family. I was there to confront the insane insinuation that clothing *invites* rape or sexual assault. This was partially about identity politics, because I wanted to be surrounded by others who had shared my experience. However, SlutWalk goes beyond simple identity politics, beyond a monologic voice of "me" or an autobiographical "utterance," to a dynamic, community space of discourse on the topics of sexual assault, rape, and slut shaming. In a sense, revising "slut," within a diversity of so-called "slut" world-views provide an opportunity to challenge the "way things are done around here." Not only do we have an occasion to challenge the rhetoric, but also the cultural, ideological, and social norms that encourage victim blaming and slut shaming. SlutWalk challenges the singular understanding of what constitutes a "slut." As the literary scholar Bakhtin correctly pointed out in "Discourse of the Novel," the problem with monologic language is that it limits linguistic definition and narrows concepts of "truth":

> We are talking language not as a system of abstract grammatical categories, but rather language conceived as ideologically saturated, language as a world view, even as a concrete opinion, insuring a maximum of mutual understandings in all spheres of ideological life. Thus a unitary language gives expression to forces working toward concrete verbal and ideological unification and centralization, which develop in vital connection with the processes of sociopolitical and cultural centralization .... "The one language of truth"...[63]

---

[63] Bakhtin, M.M. *The Dialogic Imagination*. Ed. Michael Holquist. Trans. Caryl Emerson and Michael Holquist. Austin, Texas: University of Texas Press. 1981. P. 271. Print.

SlutWalk's effort to challenge the concept of slut, and the rhetoric of rape relies also upon a collective effort to rob the word "slut" from embedded universal assumptions, or truths regarding what constitutes a slut and what actions, realities a "slut" deserves for being crowned a slut. As a practical act, the SlutWalk protest encourages this active redefinition of the term and idea of slut using what Kenneth Burke calls the "Double Process."[64] In his 1970 essay "On Words and the Word," Burke explained how words that are used to convey truths or "universals" are simply terms taken from everyday life and then assigned "supernatural" qualities; this is an upward process of definition.[65] By applying a "downward" process, that is taking ownership of a term and plunging it back into the chaotic and messy real world of use and actuality, we can transform the word, allowing the term to meet new challenges in practice and use.[66] This double process allows people to ask, regarding slutty world-views, what makes a slut anyway? Stilettos? Short skirts? Shirts showing cleavage? A skirt showing a woman's ankles? Victoria Secret bras? An athletic uniform? I was at SlutWalk because when I was child, I was deemed a slut for wearing my team's cross-country outfit without so-called "proper" underclothing: a bra. I was there because I have experienced how people are blamed for rape via the slut-shaming rationale, shifting "the burden of prevention from the perpetrator onto the victim."[67] Keeping many rape survivors voiceless.

Those who have been raped, molested, or otherwise violated hold their story close, often maintaining silence.

---

[64] Burke, Kenneth. "On Words and the Word." *The Rhetoric of Religion: Studies in Logology*. Berkeley, CA: University of California Press, 1970. Pp. 7-42. Print

[65] Ibid, P. 15.

[66] Ibid. P. 10.

[67] NA. "FAQs, Examples of Blaming and Shaming and General Lnks." *SlutWalk Seattle*. 2 October 2012. Web. 5 October 2012.

Silence is sustained for many reasons, but it is interesting to note that victim blaming and slut shaming are techniques used to keep victims silent. After all, if we make the victim the guilty party, then where is the victimization? As a therapeutic act, many at SlutWalk offered their stories in order to inspire, to heal, to inform others, and become active advocates for self. Silence is a passive agreement to the *status quo* of things, and to break the silence is to challenge the hegemonic, ideological arrangement found in slut shaming. Like many in the audience I too had a story, but not a microphone that day; yet my presence acted as a bullhorn.

I often feel I am using a bullhorn when I tell people I was raped as a child and also as a young adult. Those who hear this news become generally uncomfortable, and more often than not offer a horrified reaction to the news. A child being raped is somehow more unthinkable than the rape of an adult, yet both situations can be devastating. Statistically the youth are more likely abused in this fashion than adults. The *National Center on Child Abuse* claims that there are approximately 100,000 cases of child sexual abuse a year in the United States alone.[68] This statistic is important in relation to the fact that I used to think people's discomfort and horror regarding my confession of sexual assault was because such things were rather unusual ... "aren't they," I thought? But as the protest demonstrated for me, and for the others in attendance, being raped and sexually assaulted, as a child or an adult, is really a very common story. One in six women will be raped and/or sexually assaulted; this is not a small portion of the populace. I was repeatedly raped by my uncle as a child and later molested in junior high school, late 1970s, by a bunch of young boys on my cross-county team. Although the repeated rapes by my uncle were horrible, I often reflect more on what happened in

---

[68] Rayburn, Corey. "Better Dead than R(ap)ed?: The Patriarchal Rhetoric Driving Capital Rape Statues." *St. John's Law Review*. Vol. 78: Issue 4, Article 4. P. 1125. Print.

seventh grade, because of the public nature of the "slut shaming" placed upon me by my school, by law officials, and many of my peers. It all started one day after a sporting meet, while I was waiting in front of the school for Mom to pick me up. I remember walking back and forth along a curved pickup/drop-off driveway in front of my junior high school, practicing a song I was learning in choir. Mom was a bit late in picking me up, but that did not trouble me. I was content to wait. Not long after my vigil began, three boys from my cross-country team came out as asked me what I was doing. I told them I was waiting for my mom, and started to talk about the race earlier in the day. The next series of events are a bit blurry, but I remember several points very well: the young men started to tease me as they circled around me. One boy started the "slap game," ironically known as "Hot Hands," where you try to slap the person on the knuckles, while the other person tries to miss the slap before it hits. Another guy started to tickle me from behind and before I knew it, I was on the ground, being held down, while they put their hands up my shirt and down my running shorts. I screamed. I said no and stop, as I had been instructed to do by my mom. My heart beat loudly in my chest, as I yelled for them to get off, but they would not. They said I liked it. They said I wanted it. One guy put his hand over my mouth and then, thanks goodness, a car was heard. It was my mom with a neighbor of ours, a slightly older girl than myself who lived next door. The boys scurried. I struggled up to my feet, picked up my stuff and got in the car. I started to cry immediately and I explained what happened. Mom and our friend were wonderful and helpful. I got all the love and support anyone could wish for at a moment like that, but I was also told I had to go in and report what happened. I did not want to report the event. I was scared to confront this and I wanted it to just go away. Besides, I protested, I had a hair appointment that I did not want to miss. I had saved up my money for my first perm. But no … I had to tell what happened to my cross-country team coach, and later to the police. The car was turned around, my team coach was found, and I told him what happened to me with Mom, lending her support, standing by my side.

Before SlutWalk, I had been reflecting on that day so far in my past and I'd come across a tweet on Twitter urging me to sign a petition asking that Dan Rottenberg, editor of *Broad St. Review*, Philadelphia, PA, step down from his position because of an article he had written: "What Should Women Do." Indeed, Twitter had been alive with tweets about Rottenberg for several days:

- ◆ *@TallieBear*: #TFFs Wonder how Dan Rottenb(e)rg justifies nuns, senior citizens, or women in niqabs being raped.[69]
- ◆ *@thespindleshay*: Earth to Dan Rottenberg - women have boobs. Get the fuck over it. http://tinyurl.com/6exkfep.[70]
- ◆ *@Luna_Searles*: Part of me wants to punch Dan Rottenberg. I admit it. The other part feels really sorry for his defense lawyer in his upcoming rape trial.[71]
- ◆ *@ThinkQuestion*: Thank you, Dan Rottenberg. You've just shown everyone why Philadelphia

---

[69] Tallulah. (@TallieBear). "#TFFs Wonder how Dan Rottenb(e)rg justifies nuns, senior citizens, or women in niqabs being raped." 18 June 2011, 9:20 PM, Tweet.
[70] Spindleshay, The. (@thespindleshay). "Earth to Dan Rottenberg - women have boobs. Get the fuck over it. http://tinyurl.com/6exkfep." 18 June 2011, 5:43 PM, Tweet.
[71] Luna. (@Luna_Searles). "Part of me wants to punch Dan Rottenberg. I admit it. The other part feels really sorry for his defense lawyer in his upcoming rape trial." 18 June 2011, 11:51 AM, Tweet.

needs slutwalk now! http://t.co/K2PvtFK via *@slutwalkphilly.*[72]

What on earth did Rottenberg do to deserve this anger from such a large, diverse public of people? He argued that the reporter, Lara Logan who was brutally raped by a crowd in Egypt when covering the Egyptian uprise and liberation, deserved what she got because she did not take correct "precautions" to protect herself before the sexual violation.[73] What precautions did Rottenberg suggest Logan take? Should she have had better self-defense classes? No. Should she have been part of a "buddy" system for protection? No. Rather, under the heading of "Logan's Cleavage," Rottenberg, referring to a publicity picture once taken of Logan, wherein she is wearing a nice but slightly low cut dress, writes: "but having stumbled across a CBS publicity photo for Lara Logan …, I can't help thinking that women also need to take sensible precautions before they're victimized."[74] The logos in this pronouncement is baffling on many counts. First, Rottenberg's logic suggests that had she never worn the dress, not taken the PR shot in that particular dress, she would not have been raped. If we are to believe his editorial conclusions, then we must assume that the men who raped Logan knew of the CBS photo, had seen the PR photo and made the connection that

---

[72] NA. (@ThinkQuestion). "Thank you, Dan Rottenberg. You've just shown everyone why Philadelphia needs slutwalk now! http://t.co/K2PvtFK via @slutwalkphilly." 18 June 2011, 9:30 AM, Twitter.

[73] On July 5, 2011, Rottenberg offered a formal apology on his website, "Mea Culpa": "Let me face up to what's been keeping me awake nights these past weeks: My advice to women about how to deal with predatory males was ignorant, insensitive and hurtful, not to mention useless." Rottenberg, Dan. "Mea Culpa." *The Broad Street Review*. 5 July 2011. Web. 13 May 2012.

[74] Rottenburg, Dan. "What Women Should Do." *Broad St. Review*. 6 June 2011. Web. 20 June 2011.

this American reporter, in the middle of the Egyptian protest, was the same woman in the sexy dress, a dress with an invitation written all over it: please, rape me. Next we must assume that the act of rape was premeditated and intentional, rather than a spontaneous act of violence in a politically and socially heightened environment. Of course, Rottenberg knows all of this since he had interviewed the men ... right? Wrong.

The truth is Rottenberg had no idea who the men were or why they raped Logan, but I can guarantee it was not because of the PR shot, and it was not because she had breasts. Most women do and as *@thespindleshay* states in the above tweet: "get over it." For Rottenberg, as it is for many who wish to keep women's sexuality under the thumb of hegemonic power arrangements, blame must not reside with the rapist, but the woman who was assaulted. A woman must be responsible for what happens to her, not the man, in this case Rottenberg is speaking very specifically about the masculine gender. His logic actually argues that a man cannot be held responsible in the light of a woman's presence: "Earth to liberated women: When you display legs, thighs or cleavage, some liberated men will see it as a sign that you feel good about yourself and your sexuality. But most men will see it as a sign that you want to get laid."[75] It is truly sad how Rottenberg has such little esteem for his fellow males and their ability to constrain sexual urges. Yet he is not alone since this disdain and fear that women's sexuality will control, nay does control men's ability to act and think is not only common, but historic.

Let me go back to my history - that day back in junior high school. After reporting what had happened to me, several events occurred. First, my cross-country coach reported what occurred to the school authorities, including the principal. The police were also called in, and I was asked to recount my story again. I knew I had done nothing wrong, and the young men

---

[75] Ibid.

in question had known they were in the wrong, since bribes arrived my way the next day at school. One of the boys said sorry and wrote a note of apology. Another one of the kids offered to buy my lunch for the rest of the year, and the last young man gave me an expensive jade necklace in hopes I'd keep my mouth shut. I took no bribes, although the necklace was tempting to a young girl in seventh grade; I rejected them all. I did not want to have to talk about what had happened with anyone, but I also did not want their gifts in exchange for my forgiveness, my silence. I was angry, and I felt ... wrong(ed); I also felt powerless as the victim blaming and slut shaming spread school wide. A rumor started the very next day at school that my underwear was found in the upper athletic field, my bra in the lower - how easily I had given them up. All sorts of stories were passed around, but the ones that stuck were those two little gems. Indeed, the stories would hound me until I left Arizona: the phantom upper field underwear, and the nickname One-Boob-Becky. Kids are ever-so "kind," are they not?

What impressed me about this event the most was that although the boys had shown clear signs of being guilty, it was I who was accused of wrong doing by the school administration and the local police department when they drilled me about my clothing choices. After my coach had properly notified authorities, and kicked the boys off the team, I was called in, this time without my mom, and asked a lot of questions. I have a slight memory of being told that one or two of the boys in trouble came from influential families in Tucson, but I cannot be entirely sure on that account. If they were, I had no idea at the time, but it makes sense, the need to keep things quiet? What I remember of that incident were the type of questions they asked me. Yes, they asked me what happened exactly, and I told them what I had told my mom and my coach. Then they asked me questions that passive aggressively suggested that I was at fault in this sexual assault.

Here is how my fruitful and somewhat twisted adult imagination wishes the interview went:

"Please tell us what you were wearing, Becky."

"My club furry outfit - a horny chipmunk costume.[76] My character's name is Fido Park Avenue. You know how to find your stripper name don't you, don't you Principal and officers of the law? It's the name of your pet and the name of the first street you ever lived on."

"Ok . . . Becky, please take this seriously. Now, I know this might be embarrassing but ... were you wearing underwear?"

"Of course, my *Wonder Woman* Underoos.[77] They are so HOOOOOT and they go up my ass too. I would let you see, but I am not gonna offer you my consent. OMG, did you see that? Officer, what's under there?"

"Under where?"

"Ha ha ha ha - I made you say underwear! Ha ha ha. You're a slut now too! Dirty mouth!"

"Let's move on, shall we? What about a bra?"

"You mean the over-the-shoulder-boulder-holder? Hell no, I am a liberated 7th grader. Mom burned her bra and I followed her lead. As for your questions, why not ask those fucking boys if wearing underwear helps them want to attack a girl. Or maybe the fact that they have to wear a jock strap ... that does it to them, right? Bet you didn't bother to ask them such asinine questions. I'm fucking out of here, and you will be speaking to our lawyer as soon as my mom finds out the crap you just pulled on a thirteen year old child who had no parental representation."

Clearly, that little rant came out of a replay fantasy place where I get to rewrite the scene and embarrass those who

---

[76] Wikipedia contributors. "Furry fandom." *Wikipedia, The Free Encyclopedia*, 24 June 2011. Web. 14 July 2011.
[77] Wikipedia contributors. "Underoos." *Wikipedia, The Free Encyclopedia*, 3 July 2011. Web. 14 July 2011.

messed with my poor young mind. The real conversation went more like this:

"Please tell us what you were wearing, Becky."

"My team uniform. The shirt and running shorts."

"Ok. Good, Becky. Now, I know this might be embarrassing but, were you wearing underwear?"

"Yes!" I remember answering back loudly and quickly. "I always wear my underwear!"

"Good for you, and what about a bra?"

"No." I whispered in an ashamed voice. "I'm not allowed one yet."

I was a late bloomer, as the one boob-Becky nickname clearly suggests, and I did not have a bra or really even any need of one. Yet why even ask a child these questions? Why slut-shame a child? Why look to lay blame on me because of a clothing choice, or because of the items of clothing worn or not worn, which likely could not be determined by my classmates anyway, did they have x-ray vision to see whether I had a bra and underwear on? Was a lack of a bra the reason they had acted the way they had acted? Was it because I had only the slightest hint of a breast on the right side of my chest? Was that it? Was the molestation my fault? Those questions made me feel as if it was my fault. I felt shame, deep shame. No bra ... so that means I asked for it.

To this day I am not comfortable with my body or dressing sexy. The truth is, I could not make myself take up the call at SlutWalk to dress in a proud, sexually affirming way. I have had too many men and women make me feel ashamed of my body. A sexy dress or lingerie is not currently part of my wardrobe. I do not have any matching underclothing, but rather an obsession with running bras that, as one friend pointed out to me, gives me a "uni-boob" look (well at least this time the one boob is evenly distributed). I don't like delicate dresses, pantyhose, frills, or ruffles. Honestly, and maybe sadly, I am not really comfortable with showing cleavage, curves, or too much leg. I only tend to feel comfortable in dumpy clothing, clothing that makes me invisible to the rest of the world. I remember my dear Lee-Dad, a man I loved with all my heart, making my sister and I bend over whenever we were wearing suspiciously short shorts or a skirt. We had to pass the "test": if our butt even suggested it might show itself, we had to change clothing. I used to tell this as a joke to my friends who would ask me why I rarely dressed up. The stigma! Some friends of mine had to pass the less embarrassing "fingertip test": if the shorts or skirt hem of the outfit reached your fingertips when your hands were at your side, then the outfit was deemed permissible. Regardless, a message was being passed to me, to us girls generally about our bodies and our clothing choices: There is something I need to be ashamed of. Although I do realize that Lee-Dad had the best intentions in mind, if I had been his son, wearing shorts or tight cutoffs in the summer, would he require the same test? Not likely. No, we ask the woman how she is tempting the man, and accuse her of bringing harm onto herself via her choice of bra or underwear. So rape and sexual assault, as Rottenburg suggested in his post, is the woman's fault simply because a man cannot control himself. Seriously, we must wonder with this historical and persistent rhetorical frame, why on earth we allow men to take on powerful roles such as heading corporations and governments? If a man cannot control himself when in the same room with an attractive woman, how on earth can he be expected to control anything? This is a poor argument Rottenburg and others of his ilk are making for the male tribe.

Const. Sanguinetti and Rottenburg's argument regarding slut shaming is a common rationale and meme that goes back to the ancient Greeks, and is seen in present day discourse regarding bras, underwear, and whether the lack of these items, or just the sight of these items, incites uncontrollable violence: the desire to rape. Imagine this: ancient Greek women never wore bras; so does this mean that women in those times were raped every time they left the house to do

90

shopping? My god, it must! In reflection of this argument, I am reminded of the first time I was introduced to the Genevan 18th-century philosopher Jean-Jacques Rousseau (28 June 1712 – 2 July 1778). It was while I was attending graduate school at Rollins College. The Liberal Studies Masters program had me reading an array of great literature from the early Greek philosophers to their modern counterparts. With the introduction of Rousseau, my reading assignment included *Julie, or the New Heloise, Julie (ou la nouvelle Héloïse)*, 1761 (a painful read at best), and also *Émile: or, on Education (Émile ou de l'éducation)*, 1762. I read the two misogynistic texts back-to-back, and experienced numerous nights of angry dreams as a result. Dreams wherein I surprise Rousseau on the *Jerry Springer Show*, making him take paternity tests for the children he abandoned. I also fantasized that Mary Wollstonecraft, an avid critic of Rousseau and his views on women, and I cornered dear Rousseau in a back alley in New Orleans. We take him out for cafè latte and French baked goods, drilling him as to his misogynistic ways. After reading Rottenburg's article, I am rather certain that he and Rousseau are long lost fraternity brothers.

Rousseau's *Julie, or the New Heloise*[78] caused me so much pain in the reading that I will save you, dear reader, from recounting the horrific narrative and jump right to *Émile*. In

---

[78] Although *Julie* was a best seller of the time, this modern woman could not help but cringe at the themes in this "medieval" tale of tragic love lost. This text is not only a fictional love story, but also a template for how a woman should act, according to Rousseau: she must be virtuous in act and reputation. If not, she was a ruined soul, as her husband could no longer trust his children were actually his. It is a blessing that the *Real Housewives of New Jersey* did not live in Rousseau's time. Nevertheless, at the end of this fiction, Julie must commit suicide because she had loved another man before her husband, although she never acted on that love, and so her virtue was lost. The character Julie is portrayed as saintly because she kills herself in the face of lost virtue.

Émile, Rousseau exposes his general contempt for women. This book offers the reader Rousseau's understanding on how the education of young boys and girls should occur. Not a huge fan of socialization and the "good" society of his time, Rousseau looked toward nature and the lessons she presents for the education of the young, it is ironic how nature is almost always referred to as a she ... irony rather lost on our dear philosopher. In this text, Rousseau dedicates four chapters to the question of how to raise a boy (Émile), and one chapter to the raising of a girl (Sophie, who is specifically "groomed" to become Émile's wife). When Rousseau finally gets to the education of Sophie, the reader is first presented with his understanding regarding the difference between a man and a woman. Believing in false dichotomies, as first presented by the Greek philosopher Plato and his view of women as base creatures, as compared to men who are associated with the heavens,[79] Rousseau suggests that men are strong and powerful, while women are passive; as such, "it follows that woman is especially constituted to please man."[80] Our Genevan philosopher continues to reason that if women are weak, then the female sex has been designed to please and to be subjugated by men. This is achieved when a woman makes herself pleasing to a man, and avoids making her man angry. So far I have in my own imagination a loyal mutt, puppy, but no ... even my dear pet dog Max challenges me, which I personally appreciate ... well, most of the time anyway. Still, I look for challenges, not so for Rousseau, a man who gave away his five children to a foundling hospital. Although he was willing to have sexual relations with women, he was not willing to deal with the consequences of those

---

[79] See the *Symposium* by Plato, where women are associated with earth, base creatures seeking physical fulfillment, and men with the heavens, seeking spiritual fulfillment.

[80] Rousseau, Jean-Jacques. *Emile: Or Treatise on Education.* S.l.: Appleton, 1909. P. 352. Print.

relations. I could be wrong here, as the misguided logos of slut shaming suggests it was likely the fault of his mistress and eventual wife Thérèse Le Vasseur who tempted him into sexual relations. This is, after all, what women do: women "so easily stir(s) a man's senses and fan(s) the ashes of a dying passion . . . . dragged (men) to their death without the least chance of escape."[81]

Women tempt men and stir their passions to such a point that said men cannot be held responsible for their actions. Women do this in so many ways. One way, apparently, is when a young female child does not wear a bra, or public relations photos show a hint of a woman's cleavage. Maybe it is simply "her" existence that stirs this absolutely uncontrollable passion in men. Rousseau and the modern Rottenberg would have us believe in this conclusion: it is not the guy's fault. Truly, Rousseau goes so far as to demand that a woman be faithful to her husband/partner not only in action but also in image ... reputation. All friends, family, neighbors, and even mail delivery folk must believe that she is faithful, modest, devoted and "retiring." This is a must, because if "a father must love his children, he must be able to respect their mother."[82] Maybe we now know why he gave his children away: did his partner forget to wear her corset out in public? The shame, the nerve of that woman! I wonder if she was ever questioned about her underwear?

Regarding underwear, at SlutWalk 2011 in Seattle, there was a man stalking women and taking pictures and videos of women's underwear during the speeches. As we survivors of sexual assault stood and listened to empowering speech regarding our strength, being reminded that rape and molestation is not our fault, and does not occur because of what we were or were not wearing at the time, a Rousseauean man walked around and, under the cover of the crowd, took

---

[81] Ibid.

[82] *Emile*. Gardner's Books, 2007. P. 305. Print.

pictures of women's underwear and body parts. Occasionally he asked permission. Other times he asked permission after taking a picture. Several times he did not ask or seek consent. On the Seattle SlutWalk Facebook page, a picture of this invasive photographer was posted in an effort to identify the man: "Does anyone have any information on this man (or a picture of his face)? He was apparently shooting up-skirt photos of protesters, and we would like to be able to identify him."[83] Identified as an older white male in his 60s, several protesters said they had reported this man to the police, but he was released each time. Much of the conversation, outside of the general anger at the happening, centered on whether or not it was okay to take pictures in a public place, regardless of consent, of women's underwear. Did Washington have an anti-up the skirt law?

At first consideration, one might assume that it is illegal to take a picture of a person's underwear (normally a woman, since more women wear dresses then men). It seems rational, right? Voyeurism is wrong after all, correct? However, many anti-voyeurism laws only cover those places where privacy is logically expected: a person's home, a dressing room, or a bathroom. Standing at a rally in a public square does not demonstrate a reasonable expectation of privacy. In 2002, the Washington State Supreme Court (State v. Glas) reversed two voyeurism convictions because "state laws were insufficient to prove a picture taken in public was a crime."[84] Judge Bobbe Bridge stated that what the law dealt with was the question of public spaces: "It is the physical location of the person that is

---

[83] SlutWalk Seattle. "Does anyone have any information on this man (or a picture of his face)? He was apparently shooting upskirt photos of protestors, and we would like to be able to identify him." June 20 2011. Facebook.

[84] Associated Press. "Voyeurism Case May Test What's Private." *Tampabay.com*. 30 July 2007. Web. 30 June 2011.

ultimately at issue, not the part of the person's body."[85] It was further decided:

> Both Glas and Sorrells engaged in disgusting and reprehensible behavior. Nevertheless, we hold that Washington's voyeurism statute, RCW 9A.44.115, does not apply to actions taken in purely public places and hence does not prohibit the "upskirt" photographs they took. We also hold that RCW 9A.44.115 is not overbroad as written and refrain from adopting an interpretation of the statute that would imply the requirement of a hostile intrusion against a person's privacy interests. Finally, we hold that the voyeurism statute is not void for vagueness because all of the terms can be defined and given reasonable meaning in the appropriate context.[86]

This ruling was met with outrage and within months, 9 December of 2002, the Seattle City Council passed bill number 114411, Ordinance number 121026, which prohibited, in Seattle proper, the recording or transmission of another person's intimate area, even in public, making the offense a gross misdemeanor.[87] Further effort was made to clarify the definition of voyeurism in Washington state on May 12, 2003, when then Governor Gary Locke signed a bill making it illegal to *film or record* under a person's clothing without that person's consent - but once again, the stipulation only refers to a space with a reasonable expectation of privacy: "Chapter 213, Laws 2003: Revises the definition of the crime of voyeurism to include photography, filming or viewing a person's 'intimate

---

[85] Johnson, Tracy. "Filming Up Women's Skirts is Ruled Legal." *SeattlePi.com*. 19 September 2002. Web. 30 June 2011.
[86] Supreme Court of Washington, En Banc. "State V. Glas." *Find a Law*. ND. Web. 13 May 2012.
[87] NA. "Council Bill Number 114411, Ordinance Number 121026." *Seattle.gov*. 4 October 2002. Web. 13 May 2012.

area' without the person's knowledge and consent, *in a place where the person has reasonable expectation of privacy*. Enacted in response to last year's decision in State v. Glas. Voyeurism is a Class C felony" (emphasis added).[88] What is truly amazing is the fact that under a woman's skirt is not always considered a private area, in private or public spaces. Why the hell wear clothing at all? Regardless, the SlutWalk protest took place in Seattle, and so the acts of voyeurism that occurred should have been considered illegal, making the perpetrator guilty of a gross misdemeanor as well as unethical behavior. As such, why did the police do nothing to stop the man at the SlutWalk rally, since it was reported that they talked to him, warned him, and let him go on his merry way, filming more women in the crowd. It is difficult to speculate what goes on in the mind of another person, however one is struck by the irony of the situation; here is a concrete presentation of how slut shaming appears to be an embedded, accepted cultural praxis. Why did the police do nothing? Likely because they felt the women in this particular crowd, by dressing the way they were dressed, silently offered their permission, their consent to be viewed and recorded in this manner. Consider that the key to voyeurism laws is this idea of "permission." Voyeurism is only voyeurism when the person being spied upon has no knowledge, or has not given permission for his or her intimate areas to be viewed or recorded. If we have hundreds of men and women dressed in a sexual fashion out in public, some wearing sheer skirts and tops, and we live in a society that perpetuates slut shaming and victim blaming, why should anyone be surprised to find that the police did nothing about the voyeur? The women asked for it dressing that way, didn't they? What is consent anyway?

What is invasion of privacy?

My dress is not a yes.

---

[88] "Summary of Selected 2003 Legislation of Interest to the Courts." *Washington Courts*. June 2003. Web. 30 June 2011. p. 9.

Continuous Conversations: Naming "The Girls."

I asked my friends: Some women name their breasts, such as the comic team of "Titsy and Bitsy." Have you named your breasts? If so, what?

Mine were named by my best friend. Leon (the right one, from the movie "Airplane"..."and Leon's getting larger..."), and the left one is Obez. Stands for One Big Erogenous Zone.
  --Daniella G.

Not so much. Sometimes I refer to them as "the girls" but that's about it.
  --Beth K.

No, but I named my breast tumors Dolly, Pamela and Elvira.
  --Alexandra C.

I just call them 'The Twins.'
  --Kelly W.

No, but I really should as I have very ample breasts. My vagina is called Lois.
  --Amy G.

No.
  --Frank N.C.

Interlude
Playing Heads or Tails with My Diaphragm[89]

"And so it still goes . . ." I sighed, while sipping my double-shot latté.

"What still goes?" said John McCain coming up behind me—grinning brightly, and sandwiching my hand between his.

---

[89] *Harlot: A Revealing Look at the Art of Persuasion*, 1:1, originally published this essay. 2008. While sitting through endless political speeches and pundit commentary during election cycles, one would be hard pressed to miss the continuous expressions of careless racism, ageism, and sexism that is an under-theme to modern presidential elections. Moreover, with the amount of women candidates running for the presidency these past years, I find myself in awe over the assumption that the simple election of a woman to an office of power equates the breaking of the glass ceiling. As such, I felt compelled to revisit the rhetorical scholar Hélène Cixoius' suggestion that we need a new feminine language to combat both institutionalized and careless sexism. But what would this language look like today? "Playing Heads or Tails with My Diaphragm" comically and poetically explores this question. From mythological goddesses to Rousseau, the Mona Lisa, and John McCain's fascination with my diaphragm, my conversation with Cixous leads me to form my own rhetoric, while reclaiming my diaphragm from a "Viagracentric" obsessed language and culture.

"Politics as usual. Empty rhetoric. Careless sexism."

"My, my dear girl!" Pat, pat, pat came his hand on mine. "It can't be as bad as all that!"

"Can't it? You who champions Viagra over birth control,[90] stagnate, 'calm' courts over equal pay for women.[91] My dear man, can you smell the patronizing?"

"Don't you mean patriotism!"

"Hum . . . Yes, presently they do smell the same."

"So then," he said grinning once again—his shark tooth smile reflecting the sun, and blinding me; "I can count on your vote?

"I'll tell you what, let's play heads or tails with my diaphragm and leave it up to chance. Can you guess which side is heads . . . is tails?"

"Why the part that sticks up like a dome, that's the head."

"Ah yes, I figured you'd say as much. No more Viagra for you!"

And so I say ... yes, it still goes. Even today, Lilith, Biblical Adam's first wife, would be forced to leave Eden in protest ... in defense of her gender.[92] Tossed as she was out of the

---

[90] Parker, Jennifer. "McCain Adviser Attempts to Clarify Viagra Vs. Birth Control Comments." *ABC News Internet Ventures.* 11 July 2008. Web. 18 July 2008.

[91] Quaid, Libby. "McCain Opposes Equal Pay Bill in Senate." *The Huffington Post.* 23 April 2008. Web. 18 July 2008.

[92] In Jewish mythology, Lilith was said to be Adam's first wife, before Eve was made from Adam's rib. As legend has it, Lilith, unhappy with being considered the lesser of Adam, demanded equality. When denied, she left Eden, traveled to the Red Sea and took demons as her lovers, giving birth to a multitude of demon children. Adam wanted Lilith back, so he asked God to return her to him. God sent out three angels to ask Lilith to return. The angels told Lilith that if she refused to return, she would be doomed forever to walk the earth and bring forth demon children who would die by the hundreds every day. Lilith decided to stay in exile rather then returning to Adam as an unequal (Williams and Adelman 76).

garden—refusing to be the bottom half of a gendered binary. The phallus, hiding behind his savior Viagra, fears Lilith. She will seduce the phallus. She will walk right up to it, take it, and then destroy it. What use has she ever had for rules? That is the fear, is it not? She will become the Medusa, as I take the place of Lilith, both of us a Mona Lisa and a modern day 'Fatal Attraction' bitch,[93] whose "claws come out" to tear down order.[94] Yet what is wrong with chaos? Lilith is growth if she is chaos. There is, after all, stagnation in order. A stagnation that kills ... draining the generator, preferring nature to the false god Viagra. Slowly. Quickly. Without us looking, while we eat our cheese and crackers over a latté, tea, and friendly conversation. If you fear Lilith's power, her seductive nature, then be less insistent upon your order—your fine lines—your illusions of the perfectly working machine. She is but a teacher.

Yet, while embracing Lilith, am I not as well embracing binary rules? Am I too guilty? Is nature not a binary as well? Chaos. Order. Chaos. Order. Yes, I am guilty. I bare the stigmata that will kill me. My blood. Man/Woman. Order/Chaos. Light/Dark. Soul/Body. Can I blame you ancient Greece? Pythagoras? Or you, Plato? Shall I hate you for your perfections and your male-ordained order? You are not unique, Plato, though you may be famous, I'll give you that. You bought that fame. Like a teen spirit on YouTube, you marketed it in the streets, branded yourself. No ... you are not the only one. I am fighting against many Viagracentric traditions. Boxed in. My history blends with the history of all of her.[95]

---

[93] Akers, Mary Ann. "Rep. Cohen Haunted by Hillary/Fatal Attraction Gaffe." *The Washington Post: The Sleuth*. June 2008. Web. 19 July 2008.
[94] Anburajan, Aswini. "Obama Speaks on New Orleans Recovery." *MSNBC*. 7 February 2008. Web. 19 July 2008.
[95] Cixous, Hélène. "The Laugh of the Medusa." *The Rhetorical Tradition, Readings from Classic Times to the Present*. Eds. Patricia Bizzell

"I need to know. Were you right, Hélène?[96] Do women need a new language? A white ink?"

Cixous had taken John's place at the table and sat like a Mona Lisa coming to life in front of me. Watching me. Musing. Silent. Centered in my frenzied presence—sipping tea, while I continued with my latté.

"Hélène," I said hoping to move her, "Can I say black/white and not say white/black? What will this do to the 'sacred' social order? Woman/man. There I said it. What has happened? Anything? Is there change? Have I knocked you off your chair?"

"Shush . . . be still," she replied.

"Well . . . have I?"

Cixous's calm eludes me. I cannot be still. My history is sandwiched like McCain's embrace of my hands, between all the Hers and Hims. All pulling on me until I am the backslash living between the him\her, her\him duality. So I will reject the artificial hierarchies, the social construction of order, while still living in the binaries because I cannot seem to get loose. If I must live with the binaries, then I will reject the hierarchies and the absolute phallocentric nature of the ancients, and of Freud, and of McCain, and of my next door neighbor, who dreams of mowing his wife's pubic hair like he mows his lawn. We need not set such things in stone; besides, stone can be overthrown and the tower will just need to be rebuilt anyway.

"Hélène, wouldn't you agree? May I put words into your mouth?"

---

and Bruce Herzbert. 2 ed. Boston: Bedford/St. Martin's Press, 2001. 183-214. Print.

[96] Hélène Cixous (born 1937) is a French feminist writer, rhetorician, poet and playwright who in her 1975 essay, "The Laugh of the Medusa," suggested that in order for women to avoid being prisoners of their sexually defined bodies, they must take back their bodies and write from their bodies in a new female language, what she termed *écriture féminine*, and with a new ink—her metaphoric white ink.

"You may, but I might spit them back out upon my pleasure."

"Yes, well, that is only fair."

"So, are you ready to write from your body?"

"What, in white ink? I am not certain I wish to. I am not certain I want to write my orgasm. Isn't that the same as Viagracentric logic?"

"Are you afraid to touch yourself?"

"No, not afraid. I just don't want to continue tradition, to be body. I want more than body. And I want less than body. I want my own definitions. Could you please pass me my diaphragm? John's been eying it since the game of heads or tails."

I should have started here, with you, beautiful Hélène, with the ongoing conversation. For you, writing from our bodies will free us women. But I am afraid of being the mother, the body. Afraid of the traditions associated with it. Afraid that I will find myself reasserting the He-Said, She-Said script. I want to throw such hierarchies away, to mix them up in a martini and drink them.

"Can you not see, Hélène? Putting a new slant on an old metaphor does not change the metaphor. Glenn Close in *Fatal Attraction* is still the Medusa ... Lilith ... and now Hillary Clinton. Their bodies, no matter how firm, or their milk white, could not stop the Viagra politicking."

If I must write from my body, being that I cannot escape my body, it must not be from my milk. If I write with white ink, will it not blend in with the paper—consuming my words, my thoughts, my rhetoric into invisible ink? My blood stands out more. Let my blood speak. It too is metaphoric and lyrical and life giving. Let my blood speak. For with my blood, unless it is placed under a microscope or dissected for DNA, no one can tell what I am—which socially constructed gender ... man ... woman ... gender challenged? Let my blood speak for plurality. Let it be blood for ink.

Hélène, you write with your milk, and I will write with my blood, and we will rewrite the gendered script. We must avoid becoming the language of old, the language of hierarchies. If I fight against that language, I have a better chance of coming out of it whole and not compromised.

"Isn't that true, Hélène?" I asked searchingly, while watching John slowly make his way back to our table, one handshake at a time. "Please tell me that it's true. The language of the corset could kill me, could widen my stigmata, allowing my ink to run out, never to replicate."

"Don't think of a corset as a jail, but as a thing of beauty," said the press-deemed maverick, while fruitlessly reaching for Hélène's hands.

"John," I said, "I did not invite you into my skin. I would have remembered addressing the invitation."

"Shush. Enough now" said McCain, who was backing away from Hélène's Mona Lisa smile. "You look lovely in the corset, enchanting. Let me lace up the back for you."

"Goddamn it! That's too damn tight!"

"Just a bit more. There, now turn towards me. Yes, that is what I like to see. As Rousseau, that great defender of democracy liked to say, a woman 'ought to make herself pleasing in [a man's] eyes and not provoke him to anger; her strength is in her charms, by their means she should compel him to discover and use his strength.'"[97]

"To please you? I didn't even invite you."

"But you did, my dear. Or why would you have let me play with that diaphragm of yours? I think it landed on heads." John McCain smiled.

"Stop calling me 'dear,' I'm Lilith."

"Would a rose by any other name . . .?"

"I'm unlacing myself—I'm untangling myself from your words. I didn't invite you. I will not become you. Now give

---

[97] Rousseau, Jean-Jacques. *Émile*. Trans. Barbara Foxley. Vermont: Everyman, 1997, p. 358. Print.

me back my diaphragm, I saw you slip it into your pocket, next to your Viagra."

Watch him run. Can you see him? Limping forward, legs close together, protecting himself from possible castration—run, sir, run to Freud ... comfort each other the best you can as time for both of you is linear and short. I live in the circular realm; it goes around and around, never to stop.

"Hélène, do you think he saw in me the Medusa?"

"You're Lilith, and I'm Medusa."

"A rose by any other name ..."

You warned me, Hélène. You warned me about the seductive nature of the Viagra logic. I am trying to cut through, to break out, to step out from my mirrored-self, but the binaries pull me back, while the glass ceiling remains. I have a photograph of me taking a picture of myself reflected in a mirror, down the hall from my bedroom. I am seven, naked and lanky with uncombed hair. But the flash from the camera ricocheted off the glass, blinding out part of myself. Is it myself? Is it not? Standing inside and outside at the same time. And so is my relationship to binaries, to language itself. I am inside and outside it. I bang at the language, the logic. There is something seductive in the ordered. I fight with the circles and stretch them into ovals and finally into circular zigzags. Such warfare is not easy, Hélène. Not easy at all. My words have become naturalized. Sexism ... careless, as tossed away trash on the side of Highway 66 during an RV caravan. My thoughts—natural traditions. Even though I know better, and I do.

At that moment, Hélène slid our cups aside and took my hand. She told me to "break the mirror."

"What?" I asked in a whisper.

"I said ... break the glass."

"Is that wise?"

"Certainly it's wise. The longer you look at your image, the more united you may become with inflexible language. So, stand outside then."

Hélène bent down and found a rock lying by our table. She cupped it in her hands and then, like John, but not like John, she cupped my hands in hers with the rock in the center of our clasp.

"Here," she said smiling that Mona Lisa smile of hers, "use this rock."

Continuous Conversations: Naked Mirror Moments

I asked my friends: Name one word to describe the experience you feel when you stand in front of a mirror naked.

Frustrating.
    --Julia H.

Voluptuous.
    --Daniella G.

"Disappointed" ... but then reality kicks in and I remember that I'm a normal sized person and I'm pretty pleased with the whole package.
    –Beth K

Embarrassment.
    --Jolie CP

Why?
    -- Christy W.

Epic.
    --Alexandra C.

Middle-aged.
--Amy G.

Surreal. -
-Kelly W.

"Curvy." Not bad, especially for forty something!
–KD

Frustration.
--Rachel M.

DAMN!
--Amber

Ugh!
--Ilene M.

Doable.
--Frank N.C.

One of These Things is Not Like the Other

I will admit it straight out, so there is no confusion, I am no Dr. Ruth.[98] Unlike this great sex sage champion, I am awkward about sex, sexuality, and other *moan worthy* topics. I do not feel comfortable standing up in front of a group of people talking about orgasms, or how to get better orgasms for that matter. I do, however, feel just dandy about making jokes at the expense of my breasts, a moan worthy topic as well. Boob bating fits my comfort zone in a way that being an orgasmic orator never will. Thank god for theatre and imaginary characters, both of which allow me to step outside of my comfort zone. Orgasms, not breasts, were the topic of one performance when I played "The Woman Who Loved to Make Vaginas Happy" for a production of *The Vagina Monologues*, by Eve Ensler.[99] This particular character is a sex worker who only works with other women. She likes to make vaginas happy, as the title suggests. The monologue has her depicting the many different types of happy moans that accompany orgasms. I wore fishnet stockings, tall black leather boots, and a bustier that, happily, smooched in my belly, while

---

[98] Westheimer, Dr. Ruth (AskDrRuth). "@AskDrRuth Twitter Feed." 2012. Web. 29 August 2012.

[99] NA. "About V-Day." *Vday.org.* 2012. Web. 29 August 2012.

popping out my bantam breasts. I walked the stage with an unfamiliar swagger, swinging a whip and straddling a chair. I cooed. I growled. I made bizarre sounding burp-moan utterances. I looked out to the audience, exposing my inner *clit-orchestrated* celebration of sex. I was entirely out of my element, but as a well-trained actress I grabbed my ass, swung it right to left, and offered my best rendition of a first orgasm discovered in the bathroom at a Texaco gas station. My husband sat in the audience for a Friday night performance, likely baffled by this strange woman striding back and forth .... moaning:

"I've never seen that at our house."

"Really!?"

At the show, sitting next to my husband were men he did not know, goggling me from their seats. They laughed uncomfortably, but with delight. Maybe they were fantasizing about their girlfriends, wives, a stranger in the park, or a sex worker. Maybe even me in their beds moaning the cowboy yippee-ki-ay sex chant:

"(*The sound of a spanking*) Giddy-up Cowboy."

"Ouch! Thank you ma'am, may I have another?"

"No!"

In the audience, a man whispered: "I bet her girlfriend is happy!" It's amazing how many people think that when an actor plays a character, he or she must really be that character. Those who are in love with the method acting guru Lee Strasberg, the famous instructor from The Group Theatre, might suggest that my performance came truly from me: my true emotions, desires, and needs.[100] I this case, Strasberg acolytes would be wrong about me. Yes, I identify with many different types of moans, but I don't identify with the moans of a female sexoholic. Rather, my acting sensibilities better align with Uta Hagen, the great New York acting teacher and

---

[100] NA. "The Lee Strasberg Theatre & Film Institute." 2012. Web. 29 August 2012.

Broadway star who asks each performer to consider this question: what is your character carrying in her pockets?[101] Taking her advice, I start character development from the place of physical embodiment, extending from these outward choices, allowing the physical to affect and inform an emotional moment of action. I also apply the same process with sounds and other sensory cues. A moan rendered differently and with commitment can signify loss, pain, confusion, or orgasmic bliss. Contrary to my everyday existence and knowledge of moans, for *The Vagina Monologues* I moaned a grand variety of orgasmic bliss on the stage: "There is the clit moan. (*A soft–the–mouth sound*). The Vaginal moan. (*A deep –the–throat sound.*) The combo, clit–vaginal moan. The almost moan. (*A circling sound.*) …"[102]

Eve Ensler's metaphor of moaning for that particular monologue is brilliant, because the moan itself is primal and raw. Yes it can signal a sexual release, but moans multitask, taking on many meanings outside of sexual expression. While working on my moans, the Uta Hagen connoisseur in me discovered that the deep and resonating sounds in a single moan conjured a multitude of raw emotions and memories. A few of the moans that I am intimately familiar with are the guttural sounds resulting from food satisfaction, and the oddly related moans of loss or deep sorrow. Like the moan escaping from me the night my mother died. For almost a year afterward, I had dreams that she was the living dead, a zombie like being with parts of her face melting off, leaving the illusion of rotting meat pealing from its skeletal form:

"Let me go sweetheart. It's OK. I will be OK, I promise," says my living-dead dream mother (*Heart being yanked out of body moan*).

---

[101] NA. "Uta Hagen." *WIC.com*. ND. Web. 29 August 2012.
[102] Ensler, Eve. *The Vagina Monologues*. New York: Dramatists Play Service, Inc, 2000. Print. P. 34.

"NO" (*Angry, "you can't take my baby from me" sounding moan*). "God, why?" (*Pitiful begging moan*). "Come home Mom." (*Pleading moan*). Death is so damn ... final. No wonder humans make up illusions about the potential of immortality (*sexy vampire moan*). I wonder, was Mom's version of Ra keeping his eye on my moans? (*Uncomfortable, "I always feel like someone's watching me" moan*).

The other moan I know well is the moan of a Hieronymus Bosch-like garden of earthly food delight, such as I experience with excellent dark chocolate ice cream (*Yumoan! Yummoan! Yummmoan*)! In real life I also render a potent moan of embarrassment (*"Oh God, what the hell? Kill me NOWWWWW!" moan*). This type of raw sound accompanies certain life moments, such as when you pop out your first breast, notice the first hair sprouting from your underarms, or you are fitted for your first diaphragm. In this realm of sexuality, unlike the happy orgasmic vagina moaning character, I am more of an "every-woman." I fluctuate between desire, an extraordinary embarrassment concerning sex and sexuality, to a deep calling to write a skit depicting the Marx Brothers performing my first pelvic exam:[103]

One-Boob-Becky's First Pelvic Exam

Scene: A Clinic Examination Room

GROUCHO MARX

Oh, nurse. Oh, nurse.

---

[103] The Marx Brothers (Chico, Harpo, Groucho, Gummo and Zeppo) were early Twentieth Century comic vaudevillian and movie performers in United States. Of these five brothers, Chico, Harpo, Groucho and Zeppo were the most active with their brother, Gummo, becoming a talent agent. The Marx Brothers comedy was zany, irreverent, political, and always on the edge. Bland, Frand and Timphus, Stefan. "The Marx Brothers." Marx-brothers.org. ND. Web. 29 April 2012.

HARPO MARX

Honk, honk.

GROUCHO MARX

I didn't call you. Excuse him, he is just our x-ray man, he only wishes he was our gynecologist.

CHICO MARX

I'm here Dr. Marx, what-cha the problem, eh?

GROUCHO MARX

Well, it's time for her first ever-female exam.

CHICO MARX

Yes, I see. Well-ah, let's-ah open her up.

ONE-BOOB-BECKY

(One-Boob-Becky opens her legs. We hear the sound of a door creaking.)

GROUCHO MARX

That doesn't sound right. Nurse, put her down for a lube and oil as well.

CHICO MARX

Very well, General.

ONE-BOOB-BECKY

Well doctor, what do you see?

GROUCHO MARX

Nothing yet, I haven't got my glasses on.

HARPO MARX

Honk.

GROUCHO MARX

You still here? One honk for yes, two honks for no.

HARPO MARX

Honk.

GROUCHO MARX

Well make yourself useful and check for cobwebs will ya?

HARPO MARX

Honks. (Harpo look between One-Boob-Becky's Legs.) Honk, honk.

GROUCHO MARX

No cobwebs, eh. (Speaking to One-Boob-Becky) So, have you been sexually active in the past few months.

ONE-BOOB-BECKY

I don't see how that's any of your business, Doctor.

GROUCHO MARX

It's not, I just like to watch.

HARPO MARX

Honk.

GROUCHO MARX

Ah, you too huh?

HARPO MARX

Honk, honk, honk, honk, honk, honk.

GROUCHO MARX

Look, he's ecstatic! Good man. Well, I think we are about done here.

CHICO MARX

Doctor, I think you have forgotten to take-ah swab sample for the Pap-a-Smear-ah.

GROUCHO MARX

Oh, yes. Let's see. Please hand me the medical duck beaks (we hear the sound of a duck: quack, quack). Say, watch it, I'm not the quack here.

HARPO MARX

Honk.

GROUCHO MARX

Oh you think so, do you? Say, are you still here?

HARPO MARX

Honk, honk.

GROUCHO MARX

You aren't? Say! Listen, I think you had better watch and learn something. Nurse, please hand me the speculum. Ah, ha. Ah, ha. Ah, ha.

ONE-BOOB-BECKY

Doctor, what's wrong? Why do you keep saying Ah, ha.

GROUCHO MARX

Nothing's wrong lady, I just like the sound it makes. Ah, ha. Ah, ha, Ah, ha. Ok, now for the breast exam. Nurse, a new pair of gloves if you will.

CHICO MARX

Certainly, Doctor.

(We hear the sound of rubber gloves being taken off and a new pair being put on).

GROUCHO MARX

Ok, just turn your head and cough.

CHICO MARX

Doctor, that's-ah the wrong exam! What you-ah want is the Oreo exam.

(Pulls out an Oreo cookie, and licks the center clean. Groucho, Harpo and the Chico start licking Oreo cookies - One-Boob-Becky looks at the cookies longingly.)

GROUCHO MARX

Ok, where was I? Yes, I remember, the breast exam.

HARPO MARX

Honk.

GROUCHO MARX

So, it's your favorite part of the job too is it?

HARPO MARX

Honk.

GROUCHO MARX

Can't blame you there. Let's see now. Is this tender?

ONE-BOOB-BECKY

No.

GROUCHO MARX

How about here?

ONE-BOOB-BECKY

No, Doctor.

GROUCHO MARX

Well, how about if I hit you over the head with a crowbar?

HARPO

(Harpo pulls a crowbar out of his coat and hands it to
Chico Marx. Groucho takes another Oreo out of the
cookie bag and places it on One-Boob-Becky's belly.
Groucho then uses the crow bar to pry open the Oreo
cookie. Afterward, Harpo starts to eat the cookie off of
One-Boob-Becky's belly while honking. One-Boob-Becky
uses the opportunity to grab a cookie herself.)

ONE-BOOB-BECKY

(Finally scoring and eating an Oreo, One-Boob-Becky
speaks with a full mouth)

Doctor, do you really think that's necessary?

GROUCHO MARX

Fine, fine, never mind then. Let me see, now ... Say, you there,
Oreo mouth.

HARPO MARX

Honk.

GROUCHO MARX

Let's see if you have learned anything.

HARPO MARX

Honk.

GROUCHO MARX

This is a timed test.

HARPO MARX

Honk.

(We hear the sound of ticking - it's the ticking of a bomb).

GROUCHO MARX

Question one: One lump or two?

HARPO MARX

Honk, honk, honk, honk, etc. . .

(Honks start out slow and build in intensity - like a honking orgasm).

GROUCHO MARX

Really, that many?

ONE-BOOB-BECKY

Doctor, what are you saying? I have several lumps in my breast?

GROUCHO MARX

No, I just wanted to know how much sugar traditionally goes with English tea.

HARPO MARX

(We here the ticking stop and the sound of a bomb).

Honk, honk.

GROUCHO MARX

Yeah, well, we already know your opinion. One-Boob, it seems to me that you are perfectly healthy. I recommend that you eat a corn dog and buy a pet, and if things still don't clear up, well then give me a call.

ONE-BOOB-BECKY

Why should I do that, Doctor?

GROUCHO MARX

I told you, I like to watch.

HARPO MARX

Honk.

GROUCHO MARX

Him too.

CHICO MARX

Ah, you can count-ah me in too (eating another cookie).

ONE-BOOB-BECKY

Doctor, I don't understand, this can't be happening to me! You don't even act like a real doctor!

GROUCHO MARX

What do you expect? I'm a lawyer after all.

HARPO MARX

Honk.

GROUCHO MARX

Oh, you too, huh?

I wrote this many years ago as part of a radio show called *The Miss Adventures of One-Boob-Becky*. The effort was one of many attempts to better understand myself in a world of confusing gender and sexual expectations. Truly, I have been obsessed with these topics my entire life: from my early childhood questions regarding the origin of babies, to puberty's coup d'état on my body, to being sexually assaulted and raped, to trying to embrace a healthy sense of sexuality, to diaphragms and pantyhose and now, coming to terms with menopause (*Men-O-Pause moan*). Part of this obsession is a personal directive, while the other part has been forced upon me by nature and society. Nature is responsible for the biological changes experienced (suffered through?), but my peers have lent a hand by labeling me with nicknames. We do this as humans; our species gravitates toward labeling. Some labels promote respect: Doctor, King, Queen, Diva and so on. Other labels cause harm: Slut, Bitch, Cunt, and Bennifer (*in the style of A Street Car Named Desire:* "*Bennnnniiiiiiiferrrrrr,*"*moan*).[104] I have been saddled with several nicknames in my life, including: Dork; Drama Geek; Nerd; Sarah Bernhard; Silly-Willy, by Mom; Becky-Boo, Mom and Sister; Bebo, Reba, Dr. D., D is for diaphragm; and Harpo, after Harpo Marx). However, the most moan worthy of them all is One-Boob-Becky.

Do you remember that song from *Sesame Street*: "One of These Things Is Not Like the Other."[105] Big Bird would sing as he showed you matches and mismatches of things, and you had to guess which item did not belong? We would see three green apples and one red one; the red one did not belong. Or three small bowls of birdseed and one really big bowl of seed,

---

[104] BBC. "Jennifer Lopez on the 'Bennifer' relationship - The Graham Norton Show Preview - *BBC One*. 3 May 2012. YouTube. 29 August 2012.

[105] Raposo, Jon Stone and Bruce Hart. "One of These Things." Sesame Street. November 1969. DVD

the big one did not belong. Myself, as One-Boob-Becky, embodies this song. Like Big Bird's seed bowls, I am uneven. One nostril looks bigger than the other. One foot is slightly longer than the other, and one breast is larger than the other. On some people this might not be noticeable, but on me it's apparently VERY noticeable. I am that Sesame Street song.

They called me One-Boob-Becky. Boys that looked and sounded like Cookie Monster called me One-Boob-Becky: "Hey, one-boob! How's it hanging?" (*Cookie Monster Moan*). But the boys were only pointing out the obvious. Puberty hit and I had sprouted only one breast, one monument to womanhood, sticking straight out from my right side like the Eiffel Tower.

Puberty is cruel.

I asked for a training bra, thinking we could smash down the offending appendage and my mom said:

"For what?"

"For my boobs," I said.

"What boobs?"

"This boob."

"Honey, wait until you sprout two and then we'll talk about it." I turned to the ace bandage; what an utter failure that was (pun intended).

I grew up in Tucson, AZ, and it is really unpleasant to bind yourself in one-hundred-degree-plus weather. My best friend at the time, who had a bra already, scored me one but it was too big and so I had to stuff it. I went from "One-Boob Becky," to "yo, Dolly Parton" overnight. I feel bad for Dolly Parton; I feel bad that her name and being will always be associated with singing boobs ... who watches her face? We have that in common-Boob Bashing. I used toilet paper to stuff my new bra, but it gave my boob a bumpy balance. Rice offered a nice visual, but it was heavy and the plastic bag holding the rice against my skin was gross. I thought about cutting an apple in half and just popping it in a bra - but again, exposed fruit in one-hundred degree plus weather ... not a good idea. In the end there was nothing I could do. I would always be "One-Boob-Becky" to my peers until I got old and my Eiffel Tower transformed into Leaning Tower of Pisa. There was only one solution, I moved to Seattle and grew a second breast.

The nickname One-Boob-Becky followed me for years, even after I left Tucson for Seattle. When I would return to Tucson to visit my Fred-Dad, I could hear kids yelling at me down the consumer halls of Tucson Mall: "Yo, One-Boob," (*"fuck-you, idiot," emotionally stunted moan*). Boobs are strange things, are they not? We are so obsessed with them as a culture. Reflecting back to Dan Rottenberg and his editorial in the *Broad St. Review* where he suggests that Lara Logan's chest was responsible for her rape, I am amazed how we fetishize breasts.[106] They are, after all, no different from udders, part of the female body created to offer food to offspring. The proper medical definition for breasts is: "... the mammary gland. The mammary gland is a milk-producing gland. It is composed largely of fat. Within the mammary gland is a complex network of branching ducts. These ducts exit from sac-like structures called lobules, which can produce milk in females. The ducts exit the breast at the nipple."[107] After reading the medical definition of the breast, it leaves me to ponder: what happened when a "tit" and a "boob" wandered into a comedy club? They udderly milked it! Ha! Semantics? Context?

Yes, let's talk about Breasts: breasts, boobies, Winnebagos, ta-ta's, melons (all kinds depending upon size), hooters, feeders, ho-hos, bazongas, bodacious hahas, the girls, milkers, boulders, bettyboops, fried eggs, lulus, ant bites, mole hills, alps, apples, Babylons, bazookas, and bread winners among

---

[106] Lara Logan gives an interview about what happened that day in Cairo. "Lara Logan Breaks Silence on Cairo Assault." *CBSnews.com*. 28 April 2011. Web. 19 Feb. 2012.

[107] NA. "Definition of Breast." *MedicalNet.com*. 27 May, 2011. Web. 18 July 2011.

others. I don't want to necessarily talk about *my* breasts, although by default "they" come into the picture. Karl Marx said that the affect of fetishizing was a process in which we abstract something from something else, giving an inanimate thing (money, for example) power over us. Thus, we allow an object to control us in some way. Breasts are fetishized in our culture. I am continuously amazed at the power breasts hold. Winnebagos, if you will, seem to stand-alone, and I am not just talking about their perkiness after implants. In general, boobs become divorced from a woman's body, taking on power outside of *her.* Unlike some amply breasted women, I rarely have the problem of someone talking to me by way of my fried eggs (*Breakfast is on, moan*). Yet this translation-by-boob is a common occurrence in our society. I have noticed that when I am around girlfriends with large hohos, people will often speak to their boobs, hoping the titty translators might convey the conversation to the host body. This is a problem for many women, and several women have learned to ignore the fact that an individual is not talking to them, but to their "bread winners." Once I was walking down the street with a friend, who happened to have a very large pair of bodacious hahas. Directly in front of us was a jogging man who ended up jogging right into me because he was watching my friend's ding dongs, and not where he was going. The "girls" must have been saying something fascinating to him.

Likewise, the other day my lulus were floating free and easy outside of their normal jailed reality but concealed by a shirt, when a guy came to the door. While talking, I noticed he was talking to my car waxers instead of me. Ah, a first! But as I am getting older, I was a little worried that he was eyeing my chesticles, because my floaters might not float as high anymore (*deflated balloon moan*). I had to resist the urge to check myself. I feared we would both be talking to my hood ornaments at the same time. On a personal and defensive note: No, they do not hang low, or wobble to and fro (much). I can't tie them in a knot, or tie them in a bow. I can't throw them over my shoulder like a continental soldier. My boobs do not hang low (much).[108] But I digress. Regardless, I am rather surprised no one has invented some type of machine that allows a chest to talk for itself, instead of having to use me as a conduit.

Because society endorses the breast as a stand-alone sex symbol, many women feel like their breasts are stand-alone en-**tit-**ies. I once confessed to a friend that breasts were weird, and when I stand naked in front of a mirror, and really look at them, I feel like they are foreign elements to my body. She, I was relieved to hear, felt the same way. Part of the problem, she pointed out, was the fact we never had children, and so we never put our breasts to work doing what they were formed for: breast-feeding an infant. I thought this was a good observation. Indeed, if I had used them as baby feeders, I might not feel so divorced from them. Yet I thought to myself, people protest when a woman unhooks one of her hounds and puts it to work feeding a young pup in public. Consider Target. In 2011, at a Texas Target store, a young woman found herself in need of feeding a fussy child. She did what was needed, and tactfully started to feed her babe. Although Texas law allows for public breast-feeding, "eight Target employees eventually surrounded her and two asked her to move to a fitting room to finish nursing. The other employees, she said, rolled their eyes at her and gave her dirty looks."[109] The indignant gasps and screams of protest over obscenity are heard throughout the universe: breast-feeding

---

[108] For the full lyrics, check out Wikipedia contributors. "Do Your Ears Hang Low?." *Wikipedia, The Free Encyclopedia*. 12 Sep. 2012. Web. 10 Oct. 2012. Or, NA. "Do Your Ears Hang Low Sing-A-Long." Uploaded by musicfactorarymusic. YouTube. 11 July 2011. Web. 29 August 2012.

[109] Gomstyn, Alice. "Breastfeeding at Target: Moms Stage National Demonstration." *ABC News.com*. 28 December 2011. Web. 18 February 2012.

mothers, can you imagine?[110] The horror. This is also how Facebook must feel as employee's censor/remove images of women breastfeeding their children. Should a female nipple show, oh hell on earth, run for the hills![111] Never mind all the naked male nipples one can find simply browsing pictures of FB friends. Women with exposed breasts feeding infants in public are a hazard to our health, or so we are told. News organizations are alerted and restaurant owners quietly ask the offending female to leave the premises. But around the block, a wet tee shirt contest is in high swing. No one is alerted except for other excited people, drawn in by a magnetic force to observe the spectacle. Not by the beer. Not by the Jello-shots. Not by the music blaring out into the night. Not by the young dancing women. But by the wet "high beams" beaconing their presence. Here they tease you; they reveal only a part of themselves. The buttons enthrall you and beckon to you. Their power ... immense as they command your undivided attention. Ant bites or not, thank God the jumbo chickpeas are out tonight! Is it any wonder why women feel alienated from their breasts?

(*Everybody sing*) Do your boobs hang high? Do they reach up to the sky? Do they wrinkle when they're wet? Do they straighten when they're dry? Can you wave them at your neighbor with an element of flavor? Do your boobs hang high?

Seriously, I want to call attention to the fact that there are 160+ nicknames for breasts and nipples in the English language alone (*tittyliscous moan*). As a society, we are obsessed

---

[110] Eugenios, Jullian. "Time Cover Mom Defends Breast-Feeding 3-Year-Old Son." *Today Moms*. 11 May 2012. Web. 31 August 2012.
[111] Bindley, Katherine. "Breastfeeding Photos on Facebook Removed from 'Respect the Breast' Page. *Huffington Post*. 18 February 2012. Web. 19 February 2012.

with the female breast, all of us, including women. In fashion magazines, if it's not orgasmic advice about the illusive, moaningliscous "G" spot, we are offered articles on the perfect breast. Hallie Seegal, a *Huffington Post* Associate Blog Editor agrees and wrote about women's obsession with greater and bigger boobs:

> ... today it seems we women are more insecure with our size than ever. Today, large breasts wield tremendous power, and the truth is we -- women -- are partly to blame for supporting that status quo. This past year alone, 300,000 women put themselves under the knife for breast augmentation surgery. 300,000 women felt that unhappy with their bodies. For what? Certainly not for ourselves, as one major risk of the surgery is losing the best thing your breasts give you: sexual pleasure. To add insult to injury (literally), last month the FDA issued a new warning. Ladies, while the loss of sensation may be lifelong, your silicone implants may not be. According to a new report, at least one-in-five women will need her implants removed due to serious health complications.[112]

Seegal ends her blog post suggesting that women do not care about the risk of implants because, she argues, a woman's view regarding breast implants is not unlike a smoker's dedication to a habit that will likely kill him or her (*Oh the broken logic grrmoan*). Yet people who know the risk of smoking, still light up. However, unlike smoking, there are risks involved with not having ample breasts, something Seegal's post does not address. The risk is simple: as a woman in the United States and elsewhere, you will be less desired and seen as less desirable by society if you have small breasts, uneven

---

[112] Seegal, Hallie. "Letting it All Hang Out with My Boobs: How I Made Peace With My Small Boobs." *Huffington Post.* 18 July 2011. Web. 18 July 2011.

breasts, or oversize breasts (*in the spirit of "Goldie Locks and the Three Bears": This one is just right, moan*). Twin Peak prejudice not only affects one's social life, but it affects all aspects of a woman's place in society: social, business, and everyday. As Stephen Hall writes in *Size Matters*, we misguidedly associate size with success: "Even subsets of size – penis size for boys, breast size for girls, brain size (increasingly, as we gain new tools to measure it) – become crude, misleading, yet culturally pervasive yardsticks by which we gauge our lot in society, our sense of self, our standards of identity."[113]

"Lookism," a modern term coined to reflect the reality that "attractive" people receive better treatment, is very real in our society, giving many "non-lookers" a major disadvantage. Non-lookers would include those who are overweight, short, display nonproportional body measurements, small breasts and so on. Women are quite aware of this and, contrary to Seegal's argument, they care. This is why over 300,000 women willingly augmented their breasts, and why going bra-less is not an option for many women. I am glad Ms. Seegal can liberate her breasts, living without her bra (*a "Tim the Tool Man" moan*), but many women do not choose this path or want to for fear of ostracization, fetishization, or other practical reasons as well: large breasted women feel more pain without a bra, and uneven breasted women need the cover-up. I am still uneven and I find sports bras to be lovely things. Maturing or not, when standing before a mirror, I see One-Boob-Becky staring back at me. Lookism. Thank God I grew up in a world absent of social media. I cringe to think of how the "One-Boob-Becky" label might have turned viral on me – indeed, might still turn viral. This form of public hazing is happening Internet wide as young and old women alike are harassed for their boobular imperfections (*bullhorn "she has uneven titties"*

---

113 Hall, Stephen S. *Size Matters: How Height Affects the Health, Happiness, and Success of Boys and the Men They Become.* Boston: Houghton Mifflin Co, 2006. Print. p. 10.

moan). To have a better understanding, I turned to *twitter*, of course, and searched all current tweets for the phrase "Lopsided Boobs."

- ◆ *@Khadsss*: RT @reee_xo: how can @Khadsss_ say this girl on embarrasing bodies should be shot for having lopsided boobs.[114]
- ◆ *@BIClement*: that girl with lopsided boobs said how she didnt want the guys she knows to see her boobs, yet she just freely wacked 'em out on telly?![115]
- ◆ @FUCKTHISBURRITO: dear cpope, why the fuck do your boobs come out lopsided when i try to manip you? #sensitvegraphicmakerproblems[116]
- ◆ @JLK677: And her boobs are lopsided.[117]
- ◆ @turkeygotswagg: #1waytopissmeoff have lopsided boobs.[118]
- ◆ @SargentSarcasm: Girl - "You're so skinny" Me - "Your boobs are lopsided" G - "That was so mean!" Me - "I thought we were stating the obvious" #shrug.[119]

---

[114] Khadeem to di worl' (@Khadsss_). "RT @reee_xo: how can @Khadsss_ say this girl on embarrasing bodies should be shot for having lopsided boobs." July 2011. Tweet.

[115] Clemmy (@BIClement). "that girl with lopsided boobs said how she didnt want the guys she knows to see her boobs, yet she just freely wacked 'em out on telly?!" July 2011. Tweet.

[116] Sarah !!!! (@FUCKTHISBURRITO). "dear cpope, why the fuck do your boobs come out lopsided when i try to manip you? #sensitvegraphicmakerproblems." July 2011. Tweet.

[117] S., Jenn (@JLK677). "And her boobs are lopsided. " July 2011. Tweet.

[118] Allineed IsGod (@turkeygotswagg). "#1waytopissmeoff have lopsided boobs." July 2011. Tweet.

[119] Kyle™ (@SargentSarcasm). "Girl - "You're so skinny" Me - "Your boobs are lopsided" G – 'That was so mean!' Me – 'I thought we were stating the obvious' #shrug." July 2011. Tweet.

- *@Travel2Aysia*: #confession I use to be a ugly duckling foreal. lopsided boobs, buck teeth, ugly pony tails, dorky glasses. SMH.[120]
- *@Kidd_Range*: My boobs look lopsided in that twit pic :/ lol.[121]
- *@shovloves*: Lazy eye nipple? RT@acsengupta: I saw the queen of trampede today, nipples on her fake boobs were lopsided, & this I know cuz I saw them.[122]
- *@anaximandus*: Wife's boobs aren't lopsided, but if I can have more: please! RT[123]

The most active conversation on *Twitter* about lopsided boobs focused on a TV special shown in the UK, *Embarrassing Bodies: Teen Special.* In this show and its corresponding web page, breasts were discussed by Dr. Dawn Harper, as she frankly explained the normal development of breasts and how one breast is often bigger than the other *("So this is normal?!?" surprised moan).*[124] The video starts out with actual footage of women's naked breasts, something you would never see on public TV in the U.S., demonstrating the rather normal reality of lopsided, asymmetrical boobs. However, the tweets did not discuss the information offered about the development of breasts, but about the lopsided breasted woman as a worthless and undesirable woman. Acute interest revolved around one

---

[120] Travel2Aysia (@Travel2Aysia). "#confession I use to be a ugly duckling foreal. lopsided boobs, buck teeth, ugly pony tails, dorky glasses. SMH." July 2011. Tweet.
[121] .. (@Kidd_Range). "My boobs look lopsided in that twit pic :/ lol." July 2011. Tweet.
[122] Shovik (@shovloves). "Lazy eye nipple? RT@acsengupta: I saw the queen of trampede today, nipples on her fake boobs were lopsided, & this I know cuz I saw them." July 2011. Tweet.
[123] Alexander (@anaximandus). "Wife's boobs aren't lopsided, but if I can have more: please! RT." July 2011. Tweet.
[124] Harper, Dr. Dawn. "Am I Normal: Breasts." *channel4embarrassingillnesses.com.* 19 July 2011. Web. 18 July 2011.

young woman who was worried about having severely asymmetrical breasts, an "A" cup on one side, and a "D" cup on the other (*Holy Fuck! What is happening to me? Moan*). The *Twitter* response to her cry for information and compassion?: "That girl with lopsided boobs said how she didnt want the guys she knows to see her boobs, yet she just freely wacked 'em out on telly?!" The general message on Twitter was clear from the tweets: although 99% of women have lopsided breasts, such women should be embarrassed by this fact, since they are One-Boob-Wack-Jobs. It appears that orgasms are not the only thing to moan about.

(*Dog Howling Moan*).

Continuous Conversations: Male Birth Control

I asked my friends: If birth control outside of a condom or a vasectomy existed for men, would you insist that it's your mate's turn to take over the responsibility for birth control? Briefly explain your answer.

I don't think insist is the right word. We would definitely have a discussion about it.
    --Julia H.

Yes. I used to take birth control for hormone regulation, and once I stopped I made it my partner's responsibility to wear the condoms since I wanted to avoid the drugs. No condom meant no penetration, so yeah, other options are always appreciated and men need to take more responsibility in the prevention side.
    --Daniella G.

I wouldn't insist on it, but we'd definitely have serious discussions about it.
    --Beth K.

Yes, I would. It is an equal partnership, and both should bear the responsibility equally.

--Christy W.

Yeah, so that my kidneys wouldn't endure surgery or my boob tumors wouldn't thrive on hormones.

--Alexandra C.

I wouldn't 'insist' per se, but I believe I would encourage it. I think the only way we can solve the 'birth control' issue in this country is for both sexes to be equally protectable from unwanted pregnancy.

--Kelly W.

I'm okay with having an IUD since it doesn't bother me at all. If I had to be on the pill, I might like to pass that torch to my man.

--Amy G.

Not really but I would appreciate it if they did. I think that everyone is responsible for their own well-being. However if the person I was with NEVER showed initiative, I probably wouldn't stick with them as it shows indifference to their own well being, which in turn would make me question if they used protection 100% of the time with their previous partners.

--Rachel M.

I don't think so and I'm not sure exactly why I say that. I think guys are more mindless and irresponsible, so I just wouldn't trust one to take the birth control appropriately.

--Amber

My husband wouldn't even consider having a vasectomy, so I went ahead and had my tubes tied. Some arguments are worth fighting and others are not. I chose not to fight this one. If

there were something available, I would encourage him for
hormonal reasons.
   --Ilene M.

Unsure. Any risks?
   --Frank N.C.

Losing My Diaphragm

When it comes to the debate on birth control, the arguments are normally framed within one of two ethical positions: self-interest, egoism, versus the interests of the majority, a pragmatic utilitarianism. When I started this project, I started from a place of self-interest. I wanted to make sense of my experiences regarding gender and sexuality. In the end, we must live within the confines of our own skins, since it can be difficult and downright impossible to wear the skins of others; well, at least legally and metaphorically, anyway. This is one barrier against achieving true justice, because our sense of justice is often skewed by our self-interest. This is the problem philosopher John Rawls, in his groundbreaking publication *The Theory of Justice,* tried to tackle: how can we arrive at a true theory of justice, one that sheds simple egoism, the influence of self-interest? Answering his own question, Rawls proposed we should actively lie to ourselves; that is, we need to wear "a veil of ignorance," enabling us to ignore our self-interest when deciding what constitutes a "just" action. He famously wrote:

> No one knows his place in society, his class position or social status, nor does anyone know his fortune in the distribution of natural assets and abilities, his intelligence, strength, and the like. I shall even assume that the parties

do not know their conceptions of the good or their special psychological propensities. The principles of justice are chosen behind a veil of ignorance.[125]

Upon publication, critics questioned the potential/ effectiveness of a theory of justice based upon the needed application of "a veil of ignorance." At issue is whether or not people can truly strip their self-interest, considering the needs of others in an unbiased fashion. I think the answer must fall somewhere between "yes and no"; we must recognize our self-interest but then extend beyond it. Self-interest does not need to stop at the "self," and outside of living in an insulated bubble, it never does. After all, individual experiences have an uncanny and ironic way of lacking any originality at all. Quoting from the Swiss philosopher and writer Alain de Bottom on Twitter: @aliadebottom: "Take it as an axiom that your weirdest, most unnatural thoughts are by definition shared by millions."[126] How true this is. We start from a place of self-interest, we reach out, tentatively at first, and then potentially releasing our interest with a sense of abandonment as it collides with others. We leave our skin this way, allowing our interests to transform once they are influenced by other real work realities. Connecting. Problems occur, nevertheless, when our self-interest stops at our own skin; never interacting, influencing, or being influenced. That is the moment a "truth" stops being a form of truth, rather transforming into ideology. As the great pragmatist William James pointed out: "... pragmatism gets her general notion of truth as something essentially bound up with the way in which one moment in our experience may lead us toward other moments which it

---

[125] Rawls, John. *A Theory of Justice*, Revised Edition. Cambridge, MA: Harvard University Press, 1999. Google eBook. P. 11.

[126] Alain de Botton. (@alaindebottom). "Take it as an axiom that your weirdest, most unnatural thoughts are by definition shared by millions." 28 February 2012, 6:19 AM. Tweet.

will be worth while to have been led to."[127] Keeping Alain de Bottom's pragmatic "truth" axiom in mind, one of my worse birth control disasters, losing my diaphragm, was a ghastly event for me. But what if we take that metaphor public and imagine what might happen if we all lost our diaphragms ... our access to birth control? Or, what if others rigidly controlled our access to birth control? The personal, the political, the social elements in each of these scenarios are related and interconnected. Let me start once again from a personal account, and then extend outward.

Thank God I'm not the only one. I thought I was. I felt isolated in a state of absolute panic that morning in Florida. I had sex the night before; overall it was a nice evening, start to finish. Everything seemed to go well, the date with my husband, even the slippery parts of the evening where I had to put on pantyhose and insert a diaphragm was drama free. Now after years of practice and education, experience is experience after all, these acts of womanhood were well-acquired skills. Fast forward to the next morning. I woke in a chipper mood since I was looking forward to going out to breakfast with my husband. I went into the bathroom to remove the diaphragm before I took my morning shower, starting yet another episode of diaphragming hell. I'm talking Hell, with a capital "H," both mental and physical, since I couldn't find the diaphragm to get it out. The panic. The horror. My breathing quickened as I felt my ears redden from frustration and absolute disbelief: I was still living a comedy of errors with my bloody diaphragm. On my side, I bore down and pushed, trying to expose the plastic culprit of my personal hell.

(Knock, knock) "Hey honey .... ah .... is everything ok?"

"Ah, well ... (under my breath - "shit") ... I'm ... just having an issue. I'll be out in a minute." I replied, and then to

---

[127] James, William. *Pragmatism*. Public Domain Books. 4 October 2009. Kindle Edition. 4 September 2012. p. 88.

myself I whimpered: "Come on, for fuck's sake, will someone give me a frickin' break, pleaseeeeee?" I tried every embarrassing position I could think of to get the thing out: squatted and pushed, offering the image of a primitive diaphragm, birthing episode. I'm on my side and my leg is bent up in order to help maximize reach potential, "oh please, please, please do not let this actually be happening to me. Please. Shit! Fuck! Piss!" Although I did succeed in touching the outside of the diaphragm rim, I could not extract it. At a loss, I showered, cleansing myself for a confessional:

"I have to find a doctor's clinic this morning."

"It's Saturday," my husband observed.

"Yes, I know it's Saturday, but I have to find a clinic, and I have to find a clinic now."

"Are you okay? What's wrong?"

(Turning a bit red) "I can't get my fucking diaphragm out."

"Wha ... what do you mean?"

"I can't get it out, that's what I mean. It's stuck, and I don't know what to do, but I can't leave it in there!" I screamed, "Fuck! Fuck! This is just perfect, just perfect. God dammit." We located a Planned Parenthood clinic that was open:

Operation Diaphragm Extraction.

Scene: A medical clinic examination room.

GROUCHO MARX
Oh, nurse. Oh, nurse.

HARPO MARX
Honk.

GROUCHO MARX
Oh it's you again! You're our x-ray man, aren't you? Say, do you still like to watch?

HARPO MARX
Honk.

GROUCHO MARX
Well, good man. Me too. There's plenty to see this time around, I can tell you that!

HARPO MARX
Honk.

CHICO MARX
I'm here Dr. Marx, what-cha da problem this time, eh?

GROUCHO MARX
Well, it's time to go fishing. I hope you brought your tackle.

(Groucho gets out his fishing pole, and starts to prepare it).

CHICO MARX
Yes, yes. I know-ah how to tackle.

(Chico starts to tackle the patient. Harpo honks his horn to get Chico to stop. This does not work, so Harpo pulls out a long salami and lures Chico away. Once Chico has gone for the salami, Harpo tackles the patient. Seeing this, Chico gets Harpo's attention with the salami and he takes over the tackling. This revolving tackling/salami luring continues until Groucho interrupts the action.)

GROUCHO MARX
Well, that's enough of that; you'll scare away the salami! We'll have to go fishing some other time.

(Groucho takes the salami and puts it to the side).

137

Now, where was I? Ah yes, let's take a look at the patient's chart.

(Harpo pulls a medical chart out of his trench coat, and draws a big fish on it with crayon. After he is done, he hands it to Groucho who reads the chart.)

Ah-ha, ah-ha, ah-ha, I see. (To the patient) Well, it is nice to meet you One-Boob … err, I mean Doctor Diaphragm.

DOCTOR DIAPHRAGM
Likewise Doctor. I am afraid this is all so very awkward.

GROUCHO MARX
I'll say! Your initials now spell out double "D," and you can't be any more than a double "A." That's false advertising!

HARPO MARX
Honk, honk, honk, honk (the honks spell out: those are no double "D" breasts lady!)

GROUCHO MARX
Good point. He said to get yourself some falsies, and you'll be cured! (Speaking to Harpo) Say, you go to doctoring school since the last time I saw you?

HARPO MARX
Honk (shaking head yes vigorously).

GROUCHO MARX
(To Harpo) Ya? Me too.

DOCTOR DIAPHRAGM
Doctor, there is nothing wrong with my boobs; I am here because of my diaphragm!

CHICO MARX
(Chico bounces a ball off of Doctor Diaphragm's stomach area and it bounces back up.)

I just-ah checked it. Nothin-ah wrong with her diaphragm doctor.

DOCTOR DIAPHRAGM
Doctor, not *that* diaphragm. I'm talking about the diaphragm I use for birth control, you idiot!

GROUCHO MARX
How dare you call me an idiot, you beaver!

DOCTOR DIAPHRAGM
What did you call me doctor?

GROUCHO MARX
I'm sorry I said that, it isn't fair to the rest of the beavers.

(Doctor Diaphragm slaps Groucho. Groucho goes to slap her back, but she ducks, and he ends up slapping Chico. Chico slaps Groucho back. Harpo jumps up and down honking. Groucho goes to slap Harpo, but Harpo fends the slap off with the salami).

Enough, Enough! This is a professional establishment!

(Harpo and Chico lower their heads, as if they are sorry, and then each takes an end of the salami and starts to munch down.)

Say, can you tell me what happened when the diaphragm crossed the road?

139

CHICO MARX

No doctor. What'a happen'?

GROUCHO MARX

It got lost!

(The Marx brothers all laugh and Harpo pulls out a hankie to soak up his tears. Speaking to the patient once again.)

Now, as you were saying Double D.

DOCTOR DIAPHRAGM

I was using my diaphragm, you know the contraceptive device, and now I can't get it out.

GROUCHO MARX

You mean it's stuck in there?

CHICO MARX

(Laughing loudly) Oh boy, that-ah big-ah salami, that is.

(Continues to laugh).

HARPO MARX

(Laughing) Honk, honk.

DOCTOR DIAPHRAGM

Yes, it's stuck up in there; I can't get it out!

GROUCHO MARX

Well boys, it looks like we get to go fishing today after all.

CHICO MARX

Hot doggie, I got-ah da bait (Chico pulls the salami out).

HARPO MARX

(Pulling out the tackle box) Honk.

CHICO MARX

He's got-ah da tackle box (Grouch gets out his fishing pole again), and you got-ah da fishing pole! Ok, I dink-ah we're ready.

GROUCHO MARX

That's just fine, all hands on deck; let's open her up!

(Doctor Diaphragm opens her legs. We hear the sound of a door creaking. Chico arms the fishing rod with some salami, but unfortunately this only attracts Harpo who chases the pole and hook around the room.)

DOCTOR DIAPHRAGM

Oh god, you're making a mockery out if this.

GROUCHO MARX

(To Doctor Diaphragm). Don't worry madam, I'll get that diaphragm out if it's the last thing I do. Now, excuse me while I have a strange interlude.

(All actors freeze while Groucho takes center stage).

This reminds me of that mystifying night in Vietnam. The war had come to meet us that fateful day, and there was gunfire all around. I looked to my right; I thought I heard a sniper. I ducked down low, low into the under-bush. The protective under-bush took on the appearance of an umbrella. No, it was a diaphragm of rubbery resistance; it's rims and bulging dome protecting me from oncoming fire. The protective rubbery goodness resisted the sniper bullets, repelling them back along the narrow caverns from which they had come.

DOCTOR DIAPHRAGM
(Interrupting Groucho's train of thought).

Doctor, can you see the diaphragm, can you extract it?

GROUCHO MARX
Of course I can extract it. Say you (speaking to Harpo), hand me those serving tongs, will you?

(The lights fade and period themed music is heard as we see Groucho, Harpo, and Chico go in to retrieve the diaphragm).

Operation Diaphragm Extraction was successful, but it was also embarrassing. From the moment the front clerk asked me why I was visiting the clinic, to the pre-interview with the nurse, the consultation with the doctor, her consultation with numerous other doctors, and the discussion regarding the length and potential effectiveness of different extracting implements, this diaphragm visit was actually worse than the first appointment I had where I was first fitted for the diaphragm as a young lady. But not unlike the first time, after my husband and I left the clinic with an injured, useless, diaphragm we headed for Dairy Queen and the comfort of chocolate dipped cones. There is something soothing about synchronicity, especially when it is covered in chocolate.

I feel terribly alone during these difficult episodes in life. The experience feels singular, as it happens to me in an isolated island kind of way. I might have continued to feel this way if it wasn't for the Internet, and the communities found there. I would not have known that there were several other women who had lost their diaphragms upon use as well, making my experience just a bit more universal in scope. Go ahead, search the Internet for "my diaphragm is stuck," you will find blog posts, discussion posts, and other communications reporting elusive diaphragms. On one discussion board, Fishface wrote: "It's been in for 10 hours. I woke up 45 mins ago and CANNOT get it out. I can feel the rubbery diaphragm but not [the] rim except for a few times. I can only touch it, can't hook my finger under it. Am I going to be stuck going to the doctor?" Merry Jewess, on her blog bearing the same name, described a situation not far from my own experience:

> It was very archaic and earthy. I was squatting on the floor like I imagine a Native American woman would do. I reached up for the diaphragm and realized I was not feeling the little ridge where it normally sits. In fact, I could hardly feel the thing at all. More hysterics. "Where is it?" I screamed to my husband. "It disappeared inside of me! Oh, no!" My sweet husband did everything he could at that moment not to completely crack up. There was his nude wife, crouched on the floor, declaring that a piece of rubber had somehow floated from her vagina into her chest. It was time to call the doctor.[128]

This is why I love the Internet: unexpected community. I empathize with these women, appreciating their candid confessions that take me from my space of self-interest and reflection to one of community interaction and sisterhood understanding. As it happens, it was because I took to the Internet to find solace that I realized my diaphragm loss had larger related repercussions. My searches revealed two interconnected strands of argument regarding birth control: First, women should be responsible for the cost, acquisition, and use of birth control; and, second, men should have the right to decide whether women will be allowed access to birth control. The first issue became apparent when I noticed that women composed most accounts regarding birth control gone

---

[128] Fishface. "HELP, can't retrieve my diaphragm!!!!!!!" *Mothering.com.* 26 July 2007. Web. 23 February 2012.

awry. This did not include a smaller number of narratives about condoms breaking; men often composed these episodes. I was baffled by the relative absence of men in this picture, and in the world of birth control responsibility. Although the husbands in my story and in the blog post above are well portrayed as being "sweet" and supportive, I wondered why the female was generally assumed responsible for obtaining, using, and suffering the consequences of either using or not using birth control? Yes, men use condoms, but given a choice many will gladly toss the condom aside because using them interrupts the "natural" feeling of penetration, since "the physical sensation is simply not the same."[129] Although many men want to have sex without the risk of parenthood, most of these men do not like using a condom and will often shun using it, or any type of birth control that might affect their bodies specifically.[130] Yet those same men will be accepting and supportive of a woman's use of birth control. This endorsement of women shouldering the responsibility for birth control might not be a conscious rationale, but it is an assumed cultural expectation. This embedded expectation stems from a poorly scripted argument, specifically a syllogism: contraceptives prevent birth, women give birth, therefore it's a woman's responsibility to obtain and use birth control. This is a cultural assumption that must be challenged so that we can widen the scope of "responsibility." Once the scope of birth control responsibility is widened, society will finally promote ideological and financial support

[129] Friedman, Emily. "Why Are Condoms Disliked by So Many Men?" *ABC News*. 20 June 2009. Web. 4 March 2012.
[130] The fear of HIV/AIDs and other sexually transmitted diseases have a fluctuating "threat effect" regarding the use of birth control. Education, communication, and embedded societal ideologies all coincide to affect whether sexual partners consider the thread of STDs when they are engaged in sexual activities. Often the concern of momentary pleasure, or a fear of pregnancy takes precedence in this discourse.

aimed at creating birth control that men can use outside of the condom.

The second related argument that appeared when I conducted my "lost diaphragm" search, concerned legal control and access to birth control; the ongoing rationalization that political and religious men claim a "natural" right to legislate and control women's reproductive system, rights to health care, and access to birth control. These same men would gladly help me lose my diaphragm on a more permanent basis. I am not speaking about all men, that would be presumptuous and, in truth, many women are also against any use of birth control. However, I speak from my vantage point as a woman, as a wife, a former girlfriend, and as viewer of social and political climates. I have no intention or desire to attack an entire gender, but we must challenge embedded gender assumptions that promote a one-way birth control road toward egoism. This egoist drumbeat of absolute self-interest regarding birth control continues to be championed by many social, political, and religious conservatives. As it was in the past, today's arguments against free, unfettered access to birth control denies the concrete and historical need for birth control by both sexes.

Birth control, the use of birth control, and the need for birth control has always been around. Whether it was the intestines of animals functioning as a type of prophylactic, or the use of herbs and ointments to prevent pregnancy, the need for birth control has been a constant need for human beings. Even in the Judeo-Christian Bible there is mention of the *coitus interruptus* form of birth control, otherwise known as "pull out really fast before something unwanted happens." The Greek philosopher Aristotle promoted the use of Cedar oil, and the Roman natural historian Pliny promoted the technique of abstinence. Historically and ironically, almost every reference of the use of birth control, the effectiveness of birth control, and the need or lack of need for birth control has come from the mouth or pen of a man. It is not until the early to mid

1900s that women such as Emma Goldman, Margaret Sanger, and Katharine McCormick added their voices to public discussions regarding birth control.[131] These women, along with a few others, are the exception to the rule. Echoing through the corridors of civilization are male voices, male voices promoting and controlling the conversation regarding gender, birth control, and sexuality. Even today, as women work next to men, run for the presidency, and conduct international affairs; they are still subjected to the male authority regarding the female body. Why?

My question echoes that of Representative Carolyn Maloney (Democrat of New York): Where are the women? In February of 2012, Maloney asked this question to an all-male panel of representatives on a U.S. House Oversight Committee examining the new requirement that businesses, including those with religious affiliations, cover birth control for employees: "Where are the women" on this panel?[132] Shunning "a veil of ignorance" for denial, this committee argued that the real issue was not women's health, although this is where the conversation stemmed from, but that of spirituality and whether the law legislated a state's right to interfere with spiritual matters. It was partly on these grounds that the committee denied the right of Sandra Fluke, a Georgetown University Student, to testify about being a female Catholic who uses birth control, as well as the excessive costs of this health care need. Fluke was the president of this Jesuit University's *Students for Reproductive Justice Group*, and was chosen by Democrats to offer testimony before the conservative panel. But Fluke was denied, since the

---

[131] It is interesting to point out that women are often demonized for speaking in support of birth control, and still are today.
[132] Bassett, Laura. "Birth Control-Centered Gender War Boosts Democratic Campaigns." *Huffington Post.* 20 February 2012. Web. 27 February 2012.

all male panel reasoned that her presence came too late in the proceedings, and that the meeting was not really about birth control, rather it was about spirituality.[133] The panel's reply continued a long maintained double standard against women in two vital spheres of life: women have no place in the policy world of reproductive health, or spirituality. Here were men playing heads or tails with my diaphragm. Fondling it in their pocket ... offering a toothy grin of entitlement. In that moment, as personal anger and frustration seized me, and as I accepted the call to arms (Facebook updates! Twitter feeds! Where is the online petition I can sign???), I am told to take an aspirin and chill by the likes of banker Foster Friess, the Super PAC leader for 2012 Republican presidential candidate Rick Santorum: "This contraceptive thing, my gosh it's such [sic] inexpensive. Back in my days, they used Bayer Aspirin for contraception. The gals put it between their knees and it wasn't that costly."[134]

This particular uproar regarding birth control was initiated by the Obama administration's Affordable Care Act, which states that employers who offer insurance must also cover birth control as part of a basic health care plan. Social and spiritual conservatives in the United States predictably opposed such a proposition. Reflecting this conservative stance, Senator Roy Blunt of Missouri attempted to amend Obama's Affordable Care Act by allowing "any employer to exclude any health service coverage, no matter how critical or basic, by claiming that it violates their religious or moral

---

[133] Kliff, Sarah. "Meet Sandra Fluke: The woman you didn't hear at Congress' contraceptives hearing." *Washington Post*. 16 February 2012. Web. 4 March 2012.

[134] Johnson, Luke. "Foster Friess, Rick Santorum Super PAC Backer, Talks Contraception (VIDEO). *The Huffington Post*. 17 February 2012. Web. 27 February 2012.

convictions."[135] Here we have the ethics of one; the ethics of an isolated self that cannot transcend its skin, refusing to reach a wider community with diverse needs.

"I object on moral grounds! It just don't feel right to me; moral like, see?"

"So be it, oh sensitive one. Your morals shall be my morals. Egoists unite!"

This modern circus act does not end here. Not by a long shot. As much as I hate my diaphragm, these men hate it more and would toss it into the dark recesses of the River Styx, guaranteeing a disappearing act forever. Indeed, a modern Charon, Rush Limbaugh, is the unofficial ringleader of this birth control sideshow circus act. Never to be left out, this pit bull must have his say, as he rushes to the front of the stage, flipping my diaphragm in his pudgy little hands; beating his war drum chant: Slut, Slut, Slut, Slut. That's right, if you use birth control, and have health care coverage to obtain that birth control, you must be a slut, slut, slut. Say the word slowly. I employ you. Feel the smooth "S" that leads into the "L"uscious "U"tterance of the slaphappy "T" finale. SLUT.

> What does it say about the college co-ed Sandra Fluke, who goes before a congressional committee and essentially says that she must be paid to have sex, what does that make her? It makes her a slut, right? It makes her a prostitute. She wants to be paid to have sex. She's having so much sex she can't afford the contraception. She wants you and me and the taxpayers to pay her to have sex. What does that make us? We're the pimps. (interruption) The johns? We would be the johns? No! We're not the johns. (interruption) Yeah, that's right. Pimp's not the right word.

---

[135] Bassett, Laura. Stein, Sam. "Birth Control Amendment 'Dangerous,' Obama Spokesman Says" *The Huffington Post*. 15 February 2012. Web. 27 February 2012.

Okay, so she's not a slut. She's "round-heeled." I take it back.[136]

Limbaugh uses Fluke as a scapegoat for his party's ideology. As well defined by the rhetorical, social, and literary scholar Kenneth Burke, in his essay on the "Philosophy of Literary Form," the scapegoat is "the 'representative' or 'vessel' of certain unwanted evils, the sacrificial animal upon whose back the burden of these evils is ritualistically loaded."[137] From a rhetorical point of view, by sacrificing Fluke, Limbaugh can substantiate his position while purifying the egotistical ideology this warped logic is based upon: People who use birth control are sluts. Or more specifically, women who use birth control are sluts, and women who use birth control purchased with health care insurance are prostitutes ... what does this mean for men who use Viagra? Regardless, Limbaugh's logic is even more baffling once we remember that he has been married four times and has no children.[138] Is Limbaugh a virgin, willing to abstain from sex in order to avoid being a hypocrite? Not likely. Thus, maybe Limbaugh calls Fluke a slut not because she is one, but because he is guilty of unbecoming behavior, such as benefitting from birth control himself. After all as Kenneth Burke also argued, scapegoating is "in its purest form the use of a sacrificial receptacle for the ritual unburdening of one's sins."[139] Regardless of motivation, Rush sacrifices Fluke as both a slut and a "round heel," someone willing to simply pop that diaphragm, pill or what have you into her self, and then lie down and take it, rounded heels and

---

[136] Limbaugh, Rush. "Butt Sisters are Safe from Newt and Rick." *The Rush Limbaugh Show*. 29 February 2012. Web. 3 March 2012.

[137] Burke. Kenneth. *The Philosophy of Literary From: Studies in Symbolic Action* (rev. ed.) New York: Vintage, 1957. P. 34. Print.

[138] Wikipedia contributors. "Rush Limbaugh." *Wikipedia, The Free Encyclopedia*. 4 September 2012. Web. 4 September 2012.

[139] Burke, Kenneth. *Permanence and Change: An Anatomy of Purpose*. Berkeley: University of California Press, 1984. P. 16. Print.

all.[140] But more than simple sluts, women like Margaret Sanger, Sandra Fluke, Representative Carolyn Maloney and myself, we are all feminazis ... loud mouth "round heel" harlots to Rush and those who might shun such crude language for more sublime denial tactics, as was employed by the U.S. House Oversight Committee, the fount of this modern fiasco. But Rush, like this Congressional Committee, would deny culpability when it comes to playing heads or tails with my diaphragm.

> Do I have the power to raise their taxes? I do not.
> Do I have the power to regulate their behavior? I do not.
> Do I have the power to make health care decisions for them? I do not.
> Do I have the power to withhold birth control pills from them? I do not.
> Do I have the power to audit their tax returns? I do not.
> Do I have the power to take their little four-year-old kindergarten student's lunch and throw it away and make 'em eat something else? I do not.
> Do I have the power to look into their personal life and leak the information to the media? I do not.
> Is there one bit of freedom that I can deny them?[141]

Rather than willingly wearing "a veil of ignorance," allowing Rush to consider other points of views, this man prefers to drown himself in ignorance, claiming that his venomous comments are not a danger to American women, but they are. In point of fact, the language and ideology is a danger to all women and all people globally since it promotes a one-sided, self-interest truth that harms a larger global

---

[140] Various. "Heel v. Round Heel" Discussion Forum. *Wordreference.com.* 2005. Web. 4 September 2012.

[141] Limbaugh, Rush. "I'm a Danger to the Women of America?" *The Rush Limbaugh Show.* 2 March 2012. Web. 3 March 2012.

community. One could argue that Limbaugh was simply an entertainer, baiting hate for fodder. Nonetheless, his fuel, this rhetoric legitimizes sexism, hate, and violence. For Rush and all others who promote an equal but separate world of sexuality, as well as a misogynist view of gender, sexual violence against women and birth control are non-issues. Generally, women should just accept that they live in a male world, and males, being the generous and spiritually sensitive beings that they are, shall provide. Ladies of the rounded heel, *Father Knows Best* when it comes to sex, your place in the world and birth control.

FATHER
That's it! I'm going to put a stop to this, this instant!

BUD
That's the stuff Dad, pin her ears back.[142]

But father doesn't always know best, especially since "he" is not normally asked to take as much responsibility, ethical or actual, in the use and implementation of birth control. To deny culpability but to claim expert knowledge in the same breath is simple egoism. As a normative ethical approach, egoism concerns the right of an individual to take and promote actions that maximize his or her own self-interest.[143] When weighing the egoist point of view, it is important to consider short-term versus long-term interests, and possible side effects of any potential action or stance. For example, a short-term action of egoism might concern having sex without the use of birth control, in order to maximize and expedite the

---

[142] West, Peter, and Ed James. "The Rivals." *Father Knows Best: Season Four*. Writ. Peter West and Ed James. Dir. Peter Tewksbury. Original airdate: September 25, 1957. DVD.

[143] Shaver, Robert. "Egoism." *The Stanford Encyclopedia of Philosophy*. Edward N. Zalta (ed.). Winter 2010. Web. 4 September 2012.

opportunity for sexual pleasure. Unintended pregnancies are often the result of this short-term action and rationale. But unless you really want to be a parent, focus on short-term benefits for practitioners of egoism is problematic because long-term interests are often not considered, harming one's ultimate self-interest: "Wow, that fantastic thirty-second orgasm was not really worth the next twenty years of child support I now have to pay." Limbaugh's words, as well as the action and rhetoric of the U.S. House Oversight Committee on the Health Care Bill represents this short-term approach to ethics. Republicans are concerned about winning elections, the 2012 election in this case, and so they stage actions and spew forth rhetoric designed to outrage, engage, and unify their party's religious and socially conservative base. But this short-term posing has caused great harm since at least 63% of the American population, from all political and spiritual walks of life, supports the birth control and Health Care Bill's promotion of free and clear access to contraception.[144] Even a poll sponsored by the *Kaiser Family Foundation* (KFF)[145] demonstrates that most Americans, including Catholics[146] and other Evangelical Christians, support birth control coverage.[147] Likewise, Limbaugh's short-term interest centers on show ratings and keeping his name in the press. He did not consider the long-term consequences of his rants, such as angry protests and social media organized campaigns designed to

---

[144] Eckholm, Erik. "Poll Finds Wide Support for Birth Control Coverage." *The New York Times*. 1 March 2012. Web. 4 March 2012.

[145] NA. "Welcome to the Kaiser Family Foundation." *www.kff.org* 2012. Web. 4 September 2012.

[146] See the Kaiser Family report: NA. "Many Catholics Reject Church Ban on Birth Control, Condoms for HIV Prevention; New Pop Unlikely to Have Differing Views." *www.KFF.org*. 11 April 2005. Web. 4 September 2012.

[147] Moormann, Jonathan. "Birth Control Mandate Supported by Most Catholics, Evangelicals, Says New Poll." *The Christian Post*. 1 March 2012. Web. 4 March 2012.

persuade Limbaugh's sponsors to withdraw their support from his show. This social media boycott was successful, and by Saturday, March 4, 2012, the following sponsors pulled their ads in protest to Limbaugh's Slut accusations, collectively realizing that their self-interest would be harmed by Limbaugh's egoism: Legal Zoom, Citrix Success, Heart and Body Extract, AutoZone, Quicken Loans, Sleep Train, Sleep Number and Oreck.[148] Shock value kept Limbaugh's name in the limelight, so short-term interest won in this instance, but as sponsors pull out, Limbaugh's long-term interest could very well suffer.

Ideally, the well-seasoned promoter of egoism will sport a type of *ignorance veil* when he or she considers the potential of long-term effects for every action, policy, law, and even thought put forth. Regarding sex and sexuality, one could argue that notorious Italian adventurer and "rounded heel" Giacomo Casanova (1725-1798) was a long-term practicing egoist. Here was a man who enjoyed his sexual exploits, making no two bones about it, and wisely promoted the use of birth control. He even attempted to invent an early diaphragm like device, a lemon rind inserted over a woman's cervix.[149] A great promoter of self-love with a wish for long-term sustained self-interest, Casanova did some thinking ahead. Indeed, thinking ahead allowed Casanova to transcend his own self-interest, as he worked to avoid producing offspring he had no intention of caring for… I'll admit, this was in his self-interest, but it was also in the self-interest of his sexual partners and potential children as well. Unlike Casanova, the "birth control user is a slut" egoists are short-term thinkers, ironically promoting immediate gratification of their wants,

---

[148] Smith, Catharine. "Rush Limbaugh Boycott: Reddit, Twitter, Facebook Users Take Part." *Huffington Post.* 3 March 2012. Web. 3 March 2012.

[149] Rosenthal, M.S. *The Gynecological Sourcebook.* New York: McGraw-Hill, 2003. Print. p. 139.

pleasures, and needs, the same type of gratification that they vigorously oppose. Further, their rhetoric denies community health, since little thought is given to what might be best for their sexual partner, the community at large, what might happen to unwanted children born and not planned for, and what then happens to a society with potentially hundreds of abandoned children hidden away in state institutions. Thus, an all male panel considering whether or not women should have unfettered access to birth control as a part of their health care regiment, is a shortsighted approach to these bigger problems, women's rights, health care, and even overpopulation in a world suffering from severe poverty, famine, and disease. Whether short-term or long-term, this conservative approach to the question of health care is a problem, especially when the egoist cannot extend beyond his or her self to others.

In the end, the irony found in the objection to birth control coverage and its use is truly astounding, but perhaps Limbaugh offers the key to the real underlying objection: this may give women more power over their sexual engagements and family planning. In his rants, and using a line from banker Foster Friess, Limbaugh confesses that he would be happy to buy a woman "all the aspirin she wants." With an aspirin between women's knees, women could stay virginally pure, or at least preoccupied enough not to drop their drawers. But if there is health care coverage for birth control, then, according Limbaugh, women will be apt "to have sex any time, as many times and as often as they want, with as many partners as they want."[150] Could this be it then? Really, could it be this simple? Could it be that Limbaugh and men like him are simply upset that they have so few birth control options open to them? Could it be that they hate giving this birth control power over to women? Could it be that if they had more birth control options, they too could be promiscuous? Not that men are

---

[150] Limbaugh, Rush. "Left Freaks out over my Fluke Remarks." *Rushlimbaugh.com*. 1 March 2012. Web. 30 September 2012.

never promiscuous. Stephen Colbert on the *Colbert Report* makes this same connection when he warns about the creation of a male birth control pill: "folks this is dangerous, if birth control becomes widely available to men, they may want to have a lot of sex."[151] Well, if men are simply upset that they can't have sex without personal contraception, please ... give these men some birth control options. Hell if it would help, I'd happily donate my diaphragm!

Outside of a vasectomy, there is only one form of birth control designed for use by the male: the condom. The condom is the oldest form of birth control, and this sheath of protection has been made from intestines, linen, latex, and rubber.[152] The oldest evidence we have of the existence of the condom is around 12,000 to 15,000 years old in an ancient cave drawing in France, *Grotte des Combarelles.*[153] So this is it for men: vasectomies or condoms. A slim choice to be sure, but if men are upset about the lack of birth control options open to them, I am afraid they will have to take responsibility for that reality. This is not to suggest a lack of evolution regarding men in relation to birth control, but since the invention of the rubber, men have avoided birth control devices for male use. For years there has been talk about a male birth control pill, but the problem, it seems, centers on a lack of interest and a lack of research funds for such a project. A 2006 article for MSNBC, "Male Birth Control Pill Soon a Reality" by John Schieszer, typifies this issue. Quoting then Forty-year-old Scott Hardin, this article places in print what many might suspect regarding a man's willingness to subject himself to birth

---

[151] Colbert, Steven. "Tip/Wag - Kansas' Male Birth Control Pill & New York's Babyccino." *The Colbert Report.* 29 February 2012. Web. 4 September 2012.

[152] Walker, A.J. "Medieval Mondays: The Oldest Condom in the World." *Genre Author: Writings and Musings by A.J. Walker.* 8 August 2011. Web. 4 September 2012.

[153] Collier, Aine. *The Humble Little Condom: A History.* Amherst, N.Y: Prometheus Books, 2007. Print. p. 11.

control: "I would rather rely on a solution that doesn't involve medicating myself and the problems women have had with hormone therapy doesn't make me anxious to want to sign on to taking a hormone-type therapy."[154] To be fair, besides Hardin, there were two other men mentioned in this article who were willing to be active players in birth control use, since they were both taking part in the study for a hormonal birth control pill for men. But I suspect that their willingness is rather unique. Part of the problem regarding this research is a general lack of interest, which is reflected in a lack of funding, as suggested by Dr. Andrea Coviello, a researcher at *Center for Research in Reproduction and Contraception* (CRRC).[155] I can't imagine that such a lack of research funding or enthusiasm was a problem for medications such as Viagra. Regardless, the article was partly written on the work that is being done at CRRC, a research department at the University of Washington. Unlike other contraception research centers, CRRC focuses on the male reproductive system:

> The concept of our center germinated in 1977 with Dr. C. Alvin Paulsen, who persuaded Drs. William Bremner and Robert Steiner to join him and several other investigators to focus on research in reproductive physiology, and to concentrate especially on the male. In 1979 we closed ranks under the organizational framework of an NIH-sponsored P-50 center grant, which comprised both strong scientific projects and core service units.

This work has been progressing since at least the late 1970s and here we are in 2012 without additional birth control options for men. Let's face it, if more males had to play an active role in the practice of birth control, we would all be

---

[154] Schieszer, John. "Male Birth Control Pill Soon a Reality. *MSNBC.* 1 October 2006. Web. 27 February 2012.
[155] ibid.

better off as a society and there would be stronger respect and communication within the community of sexes. Rather than the promotion of egoism, we might have a utilitarian ethical philosophy that would look to maximize the good for the majority, including the potential person, the unborn. Consider modern philosopher Peter Singer and his position on the need for widespread population control in order to help end famine. Relevant to this current conversation on birth control is his 1971 article "Famine, Affluence, and Morality,"[156] where Singer examined the ethics behind a lack of contribution toward aiding the people of East Bengal, people dying of famine. Singer reflected on the fact that only £65,000,000 was given in aid at the time of his writing, and he compares this to the criticism of how Australia had offered little in aid, approximately "one-twelfth of the cost of Sydney's new opera house." One conclusion that Singer made was that population control, not continual financial aid for famine relief, would solve the ultimate problem of famine. Generally, throwing money at famine amounts to a band-aid:

> The conclusion that should be drawn is that the best means of preventing famine, in the long run, is population control. It would then follow from the position reached earlier that one ought to be doing all one can to promote population control (unless one held that all forms of population control were wrong in themselves, or would have significantly bad consequences). Since there are organizations working specifically for population control, one would then support them rather than more orthodox methods of preventing famine.

This is a utilitarian stance, one that starts from the self (financial health), but then extends away from the self to

---

[156] Philosophy and Public Affairs, vol. 1, no. 1 (Spring 1972), pp. 229-243 [revised edition].

embrace a global concern (overpopulation) rather than simple personal satisfaction (birth control is bad for everyone because it's against *my* personal and spiritual beliefs). This is not to say that famine relief is not needed, but Singer's article asks us to shift our point of view on the problem of famine and overpopulation. One can conclude when it comes population control and famine, birth control is vital. Birth control becomes the humanitarian choice and the ethical choice as well: global family planning.[157] This is the stance the *Bill and Melinda Gates Foundation* is taking as it endorses a safe form of male contraceptive. In 2011, *The Gates Foundation* held the "Future of Contraception Initiative Conference." One of the conference organizers, Dr. William Bremner from the University of Washington's Department of Medicine & CRRC, discussed one main reason for the conference, overpopulation: "The United Nations is predicting the world population is going to hit 7 billion people in the middle of this conference, and in a lot of those cases, it's women who get pregnant and did not want to."[158] Unlike the continuing conservative climate against the use and coverage of contraceptives in the U.S., conference goers promoted the desperate need for new forms of birth control for global and all gender use. Citing a study of over 9,000 men, ages 18 - 50, in nine different counties, Dr. Bremner stated that approximately half, or 55%, of those polled were willing to take a hormonal based male form of birth control. This is a step in the correct direction. Yet this effort is still plagued by a lack of interest, a lack of funding from governments, pharmaceutical industries, and individuals. There just doesn't seem to be as much profit to be made from

---

[157] Providing family planning tools and education, locally or globally, is not the same as a mandate that limits how many children a family can have. These two concepts should not be confused, but often are.

[158] Pearson, Catherine. "Is Male Birth Control Coming? The Gates Foundation Thinks So." *Huffington Post*. 28 October 2011. Web. 27 February 2012.

birth control as there is from maintaining and sustaining longer and harder erections. Indeed, this was Ron Paul's rationale when he announced on *The Tonight Show With Jay Leno that* he regretted prescribing birth control back when he was a OB-GYN in Texas: "I was also putting myself out of business, all this birth control ... They had less babies."[159]

Removing my "veil of ignorance," let me return to the ego, and focus back on concerns of self-interest regarding my relationship with birth control, including the pill, and my last go around with the diaphragm. I can relate to Scott Hardin, discussed above, and his objection regarding taking a hormone based male form of birth control that might adversely affect his body. I too would rather rely on a solution that does not involve having to put rubber, coils, sponges or pills inside me as well. Placing that veil back on, let's now consider all those women and men who cannot use current options for birth control and STD prevention. There are plenty of people allergic to spermicides and latex, the material used for rubbers and diaphragms, and even more people are sensitive to hormonally based birth control pills, injections, and patches. Yes, better choices in the world of birth control are needed for women and for men's use, not fewer choices or limited access. In our world, family planning and reliable birth control are needed not only to serve our personal self-interest and desire for sexual relations, but to help our species heal from the overwhelming woes of famine, poverty, overpopulation as well as the reality of earth's shrinking natural resources. We must look for the intersections where egoism extends to communal hopes.

---

[159] Volack, Jason M. "Ron Paul Says he Prescribed Birth Control When a Practicing OB-GYN." *ABC News*. 21 March 2012. Web. 27 March 2012.

159

Continuous Conversations: Sexual Quandaries

I asked my friends: Please share with me any bizarre, humorous, or strange moments that you have experienced regarding growing up, your sexuality, birth control, or living life in relation to one's sexuality.

When I was single, I picked up a small box of condoms (2-3 per package) while doing my grocery shopping. Going thru the checkout the young lady bagging my groceries asked if I wanted to keep out the small box, she thought it was a candy of some sort. I turned to her and answered "nah, I don't think I'm gonna get lucky on the way home." She looked at me quizzically, then glanced at her hand. She turned about 15 shades of red, [and] then we all had a huge laugh. Poor girl, she never saw it coming. She was terribly embarrassed.
    --Daniella G.

I hate to say it but my sex life has been pretty boring. Although there was that time during my senior year when my mom asked if I was pregnant (still a virgin) and doing cocaine (also not doing ANY drugs) in the same conversation. So maybe it wasn't all that boring. :) I did have a boyfriend show me his cleanly shaven testicles in the back of my car right after we had lunch at an Outback restaurant; we were still in the parking lot.
    --Beth K.

Having sex during pregnancy is awful and funny.
   --Alexandra C.

[My first] period was kinda strange. Brown not blood red and
[I] had no idea [what was going on]. At the time there were
still a few [menstrual pad] brands that required safety pins
instead of having adhesive strips to fasten them in your
panties! Blah! Having heavy flow and having to tie a sweater
around my waist in case I 'leaked'. Loving when I got on the
pill, after having an ovarian cyst removed, being able to stay
on them continually and not have to cycle out but 3-4 times in
a year!
   --KK

I guess the most strange (certainly the most confusing) thing
was the years before my dad came out to my brother and I.
My dad has been gay his whole life, my mother knew he was
as well. For the longest time I was confused as to why my
mom and dad lived together, but in separate rooms.
Sometimes my mom and dad would get separated and my dad
would live with another guy in a one-bedroom apartment. It
was weird. To this day I am all for homosexuals adopting and
having children, I have seen myself they are excellent parents.
However, with kids in my situation, I wish my parents had
answered my questions.
   --Rachel M.

Awkward would be [one word], when I recently called someone by [my] ex's name while have sex. That's about when I realized I wasn't ready to be with anyone. The coolest part was he didn't mind (or at least didn't act like it). I was very clear on why I wanted him over in the 1st place.
   --Amber

I'll have to get back to you on this one too.
   --Frank N.C.

The Mental Pause

The day I turned forty-five, I woke to my dog licking my face vigorously, with pointed concentration. My husband and I joke that our dog has OCD because he's terribly single-minded, and it can be very difficult to stop him from doing a repetitive actions once he starts. This includes anything from licking my face in the morning, to his scratching his neck, or even humping the cat; yes, he humps the cat. Finding my pup's action funny, my husband grabbed my hand and started to lick it. My cat jumped onto the scene, resting his body on my chest and staring at me, entreating me with his eyes: "why, my human, do you put up with this?" It was around 6:30 AM when the three of them abandoned these birthday greetings for other activities. I lay in bed, as my husband got ready for work. It was a light workday for me, since I had gotten my grading done the day before. I lounged in bed and read my e-mails; there was a bunch of alerts regarding Facebook wall updates and friends wishing me a happy birthday. I have lots of friends who live in different places, and so it's always fun to see "happy birthday" in Japanese, Spanish, and even the Hawaiian language. Sometimes I suspect my friends are doing something covert, telling me that the Japanese on my "wall" means happy birthday when it really means something like: "your toenails are very long and you need a clipping." I wouldn't really mind, such updates would make me laugh and smile just as much as a happy birthday message brings me joy.

Besides, my toenails often need clipping; oh the things we forget to do. My husband kissed me goodbye and apologized for not being able to spend the day with me. He finally got a full-time job after being on the market for quite a long time. Being over fifty, it's been very difficult for him to find full-time work, and so he happily trotted off to this new employment venture. I continued to lie in bed, allowing my mind to wander, reflecting on Mom when she turned forty-five. There was a very big party for her that year. Sadly, it was the beginning of the last ten years of her life. A sobering thought for a daughter turning forty-five herself: the last ten years of one's life ... the change of life ... twilight.

A few years before Mom died in 2001, she went through "The Menopause."[160] She'd been looking forward to it because her doctor told her that as her estrogen levels dissipated, menopause would stop her migraines. For this she would have given anything. But the menopause betrayed her. The migraines became much, much worse. At the time, she was living in a small studio apartment in the Chelsea District of New York City, while I was in Orlando, FL. Mom had been sick, off and on, for several years. Eight years prior she experienced Transient Ischemic Attacks (TIA), a series of small strokes. She had also just separated from Lee-Dad. My sister and I had grown and left the roost (so to speak), and Lee-Dad had announced he was no longer "in love" with Mom. He was soon seeing another woman on the side during their trial separation, while Mom flirted with a man online. Yet love is a strange beast, and the love between Mom and Lee-Dad never truly ceased and would grow again. But at the time, what a nightmare. Things were a mess for us all, but mostly for Mom: the now "partnerless hag," a crone. Between several

---

[160] Early articles on menopause refereed to it as "The Menopause," giving this bio-life change an ominous, stand alone, feeling: "You better be good or The Menopause (capital "M" and everything), will come and get you!" Boo!

small strokes, the worsening migraines, and the menopause, she felt old and suffered greatly for the last years of her life. Indeed Mom had been "booty blocked," a term used in roller derby to describe when a skater takes a low, grounded stance and stops or blocks another skater behind her with her well aimed "booty." A booty block is an effective blocking move that can leave another skater, often the lead scorer or jammer, in an impossible situation where she cannot go around or through the block, but all movement is impeded. As the Booty Blocker, you effectively let the air out of another skater's balloon. This is what happened to Mom, she was booty blocked and I hated seeing this magnetic, creatively intelligent woman deflate with pain and the change of life. As bad as the pain was, the worse part was the menopause, and the fact she did not really know what to expect, outside of the misinformation that her migraines would disappear. Inaccurate, ghost like disguised information about her reproduction system caused unnecessary havoc and fear, not unlike a derby jammer coming around for her fifth grand slam. Besides being a rather diet-killing and cholesterol inflating breakfast offered at the icon restaurant *Denny's*, "grand slam" is another term used in the game of roller derby to describe when a jammer succeeds in lapping and scoring on all opposing team members, even those in the penalty box (penalty box skaters are not normally counted), because she laps the other team's jammer. She is a "ghost" in the machine, passing and leaving her opponents in the dark, something that menopause does to many women in our society. Indeed, when considering the jammers, blockers, and the harsh, warlike nature of roller derby, this game is an apt metaphor for "The Menopause" and the cultural mess we have made out of this otherwise natural transition in a woman's life.

Roller-skating has been popular in the United States since the late 1800s and in 1936, amid the United State's obsession with dance and running marathons, Leo Seltzer[161] promoted the "Transcontinental Roller Derby," a marathon and race between professional roller skaters… Yes, there was once such a thing.[162] Seltzer and Damon Runyon, a sports writer with helpful suggestions on potential derby rule changes at the time, eventually transformed these skating endurance "bouts" into the sport that many of us are familiar with today. The rules of roller derby are rather simple. There are two teams consisting of five players each: the jammer, who scores the points and is distinguishable by the star helmet cover (termed her "panty"), and four blockers, those who try to stop the opposing jammer from scoring any points. Of the four blockers, the pivot (wearing a striped panty on her helmet) helps to lead and direct the blockers against the opposing team. On a whistle blow, the blockers from each team skate together in a "pack" and position themselves to block the soon to arrive jammer. The jammer, normally a skilled skater gifted with agility as well as speed, forces her way through the opposing blockers to score points for her team. The first jammer to make it through the pack legally, without penalty, becomes the "lead jammer," and she scores points by successfully lapping her opponents, mostly blockers, on the track. In derby, a game is termed a "bout," there are two thirty-minute periods in each bout, and each thirty-minute half is made up of a series of "jams" that last up to two minutes a piece. For Mom, who was once a terrific lead jammer, the Menopause blocker effectively shut her down for the final bout of her life.

---

[161] Leo's son, Jerry Seltzer is still active in the sport today, working to promote and encourage the sport globally: jerryseltzer.wordpress.com.

[162] Such "skate-a-thons " would last through the 1980s, with the Jerry Lewis Skate-a-Thons for muscular dystrophy, held at roller rinks throughout the U.S. An activity my sister and myself would participate in for many years during our youth.

Mom suffered all of the major side effects of menopause, and several new menopausal blockers not openly discussed in "mixed company": there were night sweats; hot flashes; memory loss; weight loss; and from the head down, she lost her body hair. I will never forget the day we realized that her hair went south. I was in New York City on one of my monthly visits when Mom called me into the bathroom. At this point, her migraines did not disappear but remained with her continuously, everyday, in varying degrees of strength. I walked into the bathroom with two cups of coffee and saw her sitting there crying.[163] Was it the migraine? Hot flashes? Bad memories … dreams? No, she was crying because almost all of her pubic hair was gone: "Look, I have no hair. There is something really wrong with me, Becky." Mom's pubic and underarm hair had all but disappeared and she was horrified. I could not help but flash back to that moment in time when I found my first pubic and underarm hair, how horrified I was at its appearance. It meant growing up and having to be something that I did not see for myself; and here we were, Mom was having the same type of experience as I had, but in reverse. Like the adolescent, was the crone mostly hairless as well? We left this question for more medical sounding inquiries: was it cancer? A thyroid problem? Maybe there was some other disease that links the loss of hair to the small strokes, and an increase in migraines? Have you ever noticed that a strong go-to choice in a crisis is the *logos* of problem solving? A positivist's approach that allows us to feel we can and will be in control of any situation, no matter how horrible it is. The positivist's approach is a helpful illusion, but often it is just that: an illusion. A posturing of sorts. With Mom's situation, we were not certain what was going on with her physically, but one thing we did not consider, since no one

---

[163] Caffeine can either be a trigger or a helpful aid with migraines. For Mom and I, coffee helps.

ever mentioned the possibility, was that hair loss was simply a side effect of menopause.

I wish I had discovered roller derby at this time in life, instead of my mid-forties. If I had, I would have donned the pivot striped panty and got to work. With agility and force, I would have made a hole, a path through the various blockers, the doctors and therapists offering their vague two cents on my mother's various "conditions," so that Mom could have found her way through the pack, winning her menopause jam. On this day, we wanted to take down the missing hair blocker: where did her pubes go??? As Mom's pivot, and in an effort to look like I was in control of the situation, another posturing illusion, I made several appointments in order to solve the caper of the missing pubic hair: one to her regular doctor, to check on the hair loss problem, and one to her gynecologist for the worsening hot flashes and night sweats. Thank goodness the appointment with the gynecologist was first, because it was there we found out hair loss was a normal result of menopause for some women: "Don't worry dear, we can get you your pubic hair back with hormone replacement therapy (HRT)." We later found out that the replacement hormones\estrogen she was prescribed, *Premarin*, came from horse pee ... would she sprout horse pubic hair?[164] Ay, there's the rub. When we got home that day, Mom's migraine was still present, but she felt great relief in thanks to the explanation of her missing hair, and the promise of a new harvest via replacement hormone therapy; this jam seemed in the bag, as we gloried in the predictable rhetoric found in the cycle of nature metaphor:

In the fall there is loss, as the leaves turn and wither away, so too does the pubic hair. The winter symbolizes a time of

---

[164] A popular hormone replacement treatment for women who had a hysterectomy is Premarin (PREgnant MARes' urINe). Mom had a partial hysterectomy when I was around 10 or so.

hibernation for the menopausal woman and her pubes; winter is a time to contemplate the coming transformation from mother to crone. The spring, however, presents new hope for the menopausal woman, since the divine pregnant horse pee will bring the pubic hair back to full fruit, with a great harvest promised in the summer. Rejoice!

As a species, we like answers because they offer illusions of comfort. In this case, the answer for Mom seemed to lay with HRT. I thought that by getting her pubic hair back again, she would stop feeling old and regain her youthful presence. I was wrong, as I did not understand then how feeling "old" had little to do reproductive aging. Regardless, wanting to help her celebrate this good news, and laugh a bit at the situation, I suggested the composition of a menopause song over a couple glasses of wine. Reflecting on *The Menopause* as a metaphor for war, we chose the WWI tune "Over There," by George M. Cohan as our melody, and renamed the song:

"Right Down There"

I know I've lost my mind, lost my mind, lost my mind.
I'm sweating all the time, all the time, all the time.
Men-o-pause is setting in, is this because of original sin?
Eggs have gone away, gone away, gone away.
Pain is on the way, on the way, on the way.
In-con-tin-ence is a bitch;
I'd rather be burned for being a wi-itch.

Chorus
Right down there, right down there, I lost my hair, I lost my hair, right down there. Oh the eggs aren't coming. My hormones slumming. And there's something wrong with my software. So beware, be prepared, no one said I'd lose my hair way down there. I'm getting older, so very older, and it won't come back once you lost it right down there.

Many feminists will disagree with this "menopause is war" metaphor. After all, feminist writers reject and take reasonable offense to the suggestion that menopause is an illness we must fight. Objection is also made to the corresponding rhetoric that labels the menopausal woman as "un-natural," suffering from a "disease," or, as expressed in the 1970s and beyond, "narcissistic women" mourning the loss of youth and beauty. Women researching "the change" generally confront two separate, dominate discourses regarding the menopause: the so-called positivist outlook presented by the medical field, and the feminist rebuttal that started in the 1970s. This was a dichotomy that Mom was caught between, and one that I am now confronting as a "fresh meat," or newbie to the world of menopause.[165]

The feminist approach argues that each woman has the ability to deal with and treat her own body, and that menopause is not a disease, a war to be fought, but a natural part of life.[166] Being a natural part of a woman's life, there is no need to treat menopause as a disease (with HRT); rather, we need to apply agility and speed by simply caring for ourselves, adjusting our diet, adding exercise, and embracing the menopausal process as a wondrous part of nature.[167] Further, to help each other out, woman-to-woman, jammer-to-whip-bitch,[168] we should all share our subjective experience

---

[165] "Fresh Meat" is a term reserved for new roller derby players.

[166] Kaufert, Patricia, A. "Myth and The Menopause." *Sociology of Health & Illness.* 4 (1982): 141–166. P. 151. Print.

[167] Guillemin, Marilys N. "Managing Menopause: A Critical Feminist Engagement." *Scand J Public Health*, 27:4 (1982). 273-278. P. 273a. Print.

[168] In roller derby, the jammer's "bitch" is a team member assigned to assist her jammer through the opposing blockers. A whip (also termed the assist) is derby move where a "bitch" grabs the jammer and propels her forward with force, helping that jammer through the pack.

of menopause, controlling the transmission of information about the process. Information is power, after all.

Organic, Free-Range Horse Pee

Scene: an outside cafe during happy hour.

ME

So, how's your week been?

FICTIONAL FEMALE FRIEND

Fine. (Turning to a male waiter) I'll have the house white and the brownie surprise with a side of Bon Bons. Thanks!

ME

(To the waiter.) I'll have the same, but with extra whipped cream.

FICTIONAL FEMALE FRIEND

So, did I tell you that Bob is up for a promotion? Of course, so is that teenager in his department. Wonder what will win out, "experience" or "energy."

ME

The tight ass.

FICTIONAL FEMALE FRIEND

Yep, that is what I'm guessing as well.

ME

Well, I too have news to share!

(The waiter serves the wine and Bon Bon desserts.)

FICTIONAL FEMALE FRIEND

What's that?

171

ME

I lost all my pubic hair.

FICTIONAL FEMALE FRIEND

(Spilling her wine.) What the hell!?

WAITER

(Attempting not to laugh) I'll get you a refill on that.

(Waiter Exits.)

ME

(Slowly) I ... lost ... all ... my ... pubic ... hair.

FICTIONAL FEMALE FRIEND

You shave it off? Doing Madonna from the 90's or something? You know, Groupon had a coupon for 70% off a waxing today.

ME

It's not fashion, it just fell out.

(Drinks entire glass of wine.)

WAITER

(Returns to the table with a glass of wine for the Fictional Female Friend. He trips and spills the wine because he is looking at my crotch.)

I'm sorry. I'll be right back with another glass.

(Waiter Exits.)

ME

(To the waiter) Bring a second one for my crotch, will you?

FICTIONAL FEMALE FRIEND

(Grabbing the waiter who is trying to quickly leave.)

Hell, don't stop there ... just bring the bottle.

WAITER

(Nervous laugh) Ok. Sorry again. (Exits)

FICTIONAL FEMALE FRIEND

Jesus, you see a doctor about this?

ME

(Wiping up my crouch)

Yep, he said it's part of menopause and he gave me a script for horse pee pills.

FICTIONAL FEMALE FRIEND

What?

ME

(Talking as the waiter returns with a bottle of wine and two glasses. The waiter starts to pour.)

Hormone replacement therapy. Apparently they harvest the pee of pregnant horses. Lots of estrogen there. Then it's made into a pill and wa-la! New pubic hair!

WAITER

Are these free-range horses?

FICTIONAL FEMALE FRIEND
Good question!

ME
How the fuck should I know?

WAITER
If it were me, I'd want to know. Do no harm.

ME
(Staring at the waiter) What the fuck ... Dude, have you ever lost your pubic hair?

FICTIONAL FEMALE FRIEND
Come on Reba, he has a point.

ME
Fine. I'll investigate where I can get some organic free-range horse pee. Bloody hell. Give me that bottle. I hope this was made from free-range grapes.

(End Scene. Fade to Black)

The positivist discourse regarding menopause places far less emphasis on female-to-waiter sharing, suggesting that menopausal knowledge belongs to the realm of the specialist, a doctor-to-patient relationship, where information is controlled and provided by the medical community. It is this approach that dominates today's discussion regarding menopause and "perimenopause," and what women should know about the so-called "change of life." The message here is loud and clear: menopause is a disease because the female body no longer produces the *correct* hormonal balance. The language often used to define menopause is sterile and distance, jargon encouraging a hands off approach by individual women experiencing this change of life:

Menopause is the last menstruation governed by ovarian function--bleeding caused by nonhormonal endometrical pathology (e.g. polyps, myomata) are excluded. Existing amenorrhea, climacteric age, exclusion of pregnancy, of intake of medications causing amenorrhea, of endocrine pathology or consuming diseases, repeated determinations of estradiol (<30 pg/ml) and of follicle-stimulating hormone (FSH) in plasma (>40 IE.I), measurement of ovarian volume, exclusion of ovulatory follicles and measurement of endometrial thickness (<5 mm) may help establish a define diagnosis of menopause.[169]

Once this convoluted definition (or definitions like this) is confronted, a menopausal woman finds she's even more at the mercy of the medical community as soon as it is disclosed that she is at a higher risk for life blockers, such as: cancer, memory loss, incontinence, cardiovascular disease, osteoporosis, loss of collagen, loss of sexual appetite and so on. Both the use of sterile language and the reality of potential physical conditions that could lead to death leave many women feeling helpless in the face of her midlife change, helpless and useless. As anthropologist Emily Martin discovered while examining the discourse surrounding the "Egg and the Sperm" in medical texts, the female cycle has historically been described as a "productive enterprise" designed to produce children. As such, when a woman menstruates or, god forbid, ceases to menstruate then her role in this productive enterprise equates failure.[170] It's hard for

---

[169] Lauritzen, Christian, and John Studd. *Current Management of the Menopause*. London: Taylor & Francis, 2005: p. 4. Print.
[170] Martin, Emily. "The Egg and the Sperm: How Science Has Constructed a Romance Based on Stereotypical Male-Female Roles." *Gender and Scientific Authority*. Barbara Laslett, Sally G. Kohlstedt, Helen Longio, and Evelynn Hammonds Eds. Chicago: University of Chicago Press: 323-339. Print.

older crone jammers in our culture, how can you be a woman in menopause without failure, feeling old, becoming the butt of a joke or the menopause myth itself? In today's world, it's difficult to do, since the positivist's discourse on menopause not only describes a condition, a stage of life, but the female as well. She becomes "The Menopause" in the eyes of a youth obsessed culture. Social theorist Patricia A. Kaufert[171] points to the overall medical and Freudian take on menopause that equates the menopausal subject (she is no longer a woman in her own right, but "the menopausal" myth), as obsolete: "the menopause can only be seen as loss; loss of fertility, loss of femininity, loss of meaning in a woman's life."[172] Because menopause corresponds to the obsolete and failure in an operational process, it is up to the medical field to bring meaning back to the menopausal subject. This idea is sold to women via fear rhetoric that argues if we do not try this hormone replacement therapy or that set of vitamins, then we will succumb to menopause-associated diseases.[173] This approach to menopause requires a woman to stop being a unique individual and, rather, she must become the menopause itself. As long as a woman becomes her sexual/reproductive life designation, she can be objectified and treated as a function rather than an individual.

- Pre-menstrual, adolescent: Maiden, female as nymphet.
- Child bearing age: Mother, *Of Woman Born.*[174]

---

[171] Patricia A. Kaufert is a Professor in the Department of Community Health Sciences in the Faculty of Medicine at the University of Manitoba.
[172] Kaufert, 160.
[173] Guillemin, 274.
[174] Rich, Adrienne. *Of Woman Born.* New York: W.W. Norton, 1986. Print.

◆ Perimenopausal: waning mother (like a waxing moon), the end is near.

◆ The menopause: This is it, we are now quite definitely going to die, aren't we?[175]

We become our menstrual designation where the resulting symptoms can be controlled by outside beings, advertisers and doctors, all who claim to know better than we do about such things. Information is proprietary as medical blockers determine the jammer's outcome.

Historically, the insinuation that a woman is her perceived function rather than an individual has a long history. Consider the rhetoric that a woman, during her period, ceases to be a woman and becomes, rather, a vessel of impurity. For example, the Old Testament, *Leviticus*, 15:19 states: "When a woman has her regular flow of blood, the impurity of her monthly period will last seven days, and anyone who touches her will be unclean till evening." Another classic example of demonizing and objectifying the menstruating subject can be found with the ancient Greek philosopher, and student of Plato, Aristotle (384-322 BC), who proclaimed that menstruating women tarnished mirrors... That's a waste of good witchcraft, if you ask me. Not to be undone, Pliny the Elder, the ancient Roman author and naturalist argued that a woman who "walks through the fields during her period will ruin the crops and wither vines."[176] Like the menstruating woman, the older, menopausal woman is also objectified and deemed suspect. For example, in the famous *The Hammer of Witches* (*Malleus Maleficarum*) published in 1489, an old woman who endured past her childbearing years was seen as little

---

[175] Adams, Douglas. *The Hitchhiker's Guide to the Galaxy*. New York: Harmony Books, 1980. Print. P. 116.

[176] Williams, Selma R., and Pamela Williams Adelman. *Riding the Nightmare: Women & Witchcraft from the Old World to Colonial Salem*. New York, NY: Harper Perennial, New York, 1992. Print. P. 39.

more than a crone, a witch, a hag, and a bitchy one at that: "[Old women are] often inflamed with malice or rage."[177]

The Hammer of the Witches an interesting text for this discussion. Historically, this text functioned to objectify and forcibly subjugate women, and it is partly responsible for the mass witch-hunt and burnings in Europe. *The Hammer*[178] also aided the process of ending the transmission of knowledge and information regarding sexuality between women, when it helped destroy the traditional function of the female healer and midwife:

> Midwives surpass all others in wickedness. When [midwives] do not kill the child, they blasphemously offer it to the Devil in this manner. As soon as the child is born, the midwife, if the mother is not a witch, carries it out of the room on the pretext of warming it, raises it up, and offers it to the Prince of Devils, that is Lucifer, and to all the devils, and this is done by the kitchen fire."[179]

The "midwives are witches" argument is one example of a series of attacks that were directed toward midwives in Europe, which incidentally also opened the way for the rise of

---

[177] Ibid, 40.

[178] It is interesting, but not surprising to note that there is "hammer" terminology in roller derby as well. When you hit an opposing skater hard, you "hammer" her. In the "hammer & nail" play, two players work to bring down a target. First there is the booty blocker who works to stay in front of the target, keeping her blocked from moving, and slowing that target down. This tends to make the skater lose her grounded skating position, forcing her to skate upright, putting her at risk of falling when hit. At this point, the "hammer" goes in for the hit, while pushing the booty blocker out of harms way.

[179] Williams, Selma R., and Pamela Williams Adelman, 40.

the "modern" medical profession and obstetrics.[180] As Adrienne Rich points out in *Of Women Born,* the ancient physician made a distinction between midwifery and the early development of obstetrics/science. Midwifery was seen by educated men as a disgusting practice (not a science), simply because of its connection to women, their disgusting and repulsive bodies, and the lack of "official" education received by midwives. What was needed, rather, was to abolish midwifery in exchange for the science of obstetrics:

Doctors and Midwives

Scene: The house of a woman about ready to give birth.

BUDDING DOCTOR

(Budding Doctor is seen trying to push the midwife away from the Mother To Be.)

---

[180] The death of the midwife as a profession experienced a long suffering end, starting with the witch hunts and ending with modern obstetrics, founded in the mid to late 1700s. Traditionally, the modern obstetrics profession is attributed to William Hunter and William Smellie. It is interesting to note, however, that although these men were highly praised by the medical community, historian Don Shelton argued in 2010, in the *Journal of the Royal Society of Medicine* (JRSM), that these two men were basically serial killers: "Smellie and Hunter were responsible for a series of 18th-century 'burking' murders [murdering for medical research] of pregnant women, with a death total greater than the combined murders committed by Burke and Hare and Jack the Ripper" (Shelton as cited by Campbell, Denis. Founders of British obstetrics 'were callous murderers.' *The Guardian: The Observer,* Web. Sunday, 7 February 2010).

Of course, I am a scientist old woman, now move aside, the baby is coming now, I must get in there and pull the child out or it will surely die!

(To patient.)

Stop squatting and lay down, woman.

MIDWIFE
(Aside) God save us from lawyers and doctors.

(Speaking to the mother, who is still seen squatting over a mat.)

Don't listen to him dear and just push like we discussed. Push now!

BUDDING DOCTOR
The woman is not having a bowel movement! For God's sake move woman, get out of my way.

MIDWIFE
For God's sake, wash you bloody hands before you go in there, you idiot!

MOTHER TO BE
(Pushing) ughhhhhhhhhh.

(Scene ends with Budding Doctor wrestling the Midwife in order to catch the baby. Lights fade to black.)

The documented shift of information about reproduction, and the position of the midwife to the "man-midwife" began in France, in the court of Louis XIV and Boucher, the court physician. Boucher attended King Louis' favorite mistress, Duchess de la Vallieère in 1663, and it is here that the man-midwife (*accoucheur*) was officially anointed, while the female as healer was dealt a serious blow.[181] This historical moment also contributed to the erosion of woman-to-woman transmission of reproductive knowledge and information, which is still true for our world today. Mom did not know about the effects of menopause because her mother, her grandmother, and her friends never spoke of it. In roller derby, this is a "no pack" situation, where the pack of blockers in a jam is either intentionally, or accidentally separated, making blocking attempts almost futile, allowing the jammer to push on through without any resistance whatsoever. Women need their pack, for without the communication of information and assistance, the bout might as well be over. In my mother's world, the medical field and cultural dismissal of female autonomy effectively blocked practical and needed information about her body. There was no discussion of menopause, nor, for that matter, was there any discussion regarding menstruation, childbirth and so on. These discussions stayed between doctor and patient, and normally occurred only after the fact in many cases. Indeed, long standing laws such as the 1873 Comstock Laws institutionalized silence between women. The Comstock Law made it illegal to send any "obscene, lewd, and/or lascivious" information through the mail, including letters containing information about birth control, sexually transmitted diseases, or reproductive aging. Aspects of this law stood in some states until 1965 when the United States Supreme Count ruled in the Griswold v. Connecticut case that the constitution protected privacy, including the privacy regarding the use of contraception. Finally, contraception was not defined as obscene or lewd! It is interesting to note, however, that this case only extended to married relationships, and it would not be until 1972, the Eisenstadt v. Baird case, where the same

---

[181] Rich, Adrienne. *Of Woman Born: Motherhood as Experience and Institution*. New York, NY: Norton, 1995. Pp. 138-140.

grace was extended to those in an unmarried relationship as well. Regardless, the point is simple: laws instituted silence, and so many women, my mom included, discovered sexuality haphazardly. Since Mom was horrified at being in the dark with each discovery, she attempted to correct this misguided approach to reproductive knowledge, transmitting all she knew to her daughters, so that we would not experience the same loss of control in the face of ignorance.

This lack of transmission of knowledge regarding sexuality, reproduction, and menopause is very common among middle-class Euro-American women. Eve Agee, from the U.S. Department of Education, Washington, DC, discovered that unlike many in the Euro-American female community, the Black American community in southern parts of the United States shared information from mother-to-daughter, and this information allowed these women going through menopause to better navigate the experience.[182] But this example seems the exception to the rule. For myself, after being diagnosed as perimenopausal, I was in the dark regarding what that meant. I had no idea how pre-menopause would be different from actual menopause. Hell, I had no idea that there was a pre-game, a tailgate event and neither did most of my friends.[183] Further, I became worried when my period started coming more often, staying longer. After all, when looking up perimenopause, most texts state that this is the time when one's period comes less and less, not more and more. Like Mom when she lost her pubic hair, I became concerned. Since I know few women in my age group, and since it did not immediately occur to me to put out a Facebook query on the

---

[182] Agee, Eve. "Menopause and the Transmission of Women's Knowledge: African American and White Women's Perspectives." *Medical Anthropology Quarterly*, New Series. 14:1 (March 2000), pp. 73-95.

[183] I have, however, attended the after party – you know, the party when you find out about all this important sexual information after-the-fact.

topic, I took to the web to find information, to locate my pack. The Twitter feeds were filled with spam like information on imaginary cures, and bad jokes: "Do you wonder if global warming is connected with the 70,000,000 women in the U.S. in Menopause?"[184] But I finally discovered my pack in a discussion community forum featuring women that had the same problem as myself, missing information about their body's processes: "Guest Posted: Sep-02 08:12 PM: I'm having periods more frequently, and occasionally I spot for up to a week after my period, making it last for two weeks. Anyone else have longer or more frequent periods during perimenopause?"

Jankeys: Posted: Sep-17 10:50 AM: I have been searching on here for awhile, hoping to find someone else who has been experiencing the same physical and mental problems regarding peri-menopause. I came across this website and was fortunate enough to read your post. For two years now, I have had really abnormal periods. I go for my yearly exam and so far, thank God, nothing has been wrong. My mother's sister had uterine cancer at 76 years of age. She had surgery and did remarkably well, and now is about to celebrate her 81st birthday! I am concerned because my periods are longer and sometimes quite heavy. They average between 17 and 26 days apart. I do spot for longer than a week afterwards. In fact, this past month, I haven't stopped spotting except for sporadic days. I think I can actually tell a change in my hormonal level. The balance is off, as I get hot-flashes that are more severe, headaches, a sudden onset of cramps that [won't] go away and

---

184 Hot Flash Havoc. (HotFlashHavoc). "Do you wonder if global warming is connected with the 70,000,000 women in the U.S. in Menopause &35 mil in perimenopause http://www.hotflashhavoc.com." 26 March 2012, 8:10 PM. Tweet.

sometimes I'm a bit lightheaded. Please let me know if anyone else experiences these symptoms. Thanks!![185]

Eighty-five women replied to the "Guest's" initial post, all having similar problems and all searching for validation as to their perimenopausal experience. Why did we all need to seek out a community of Internet strangers to find out that what we were experiencing was, in fact, likely normal? Why were we not told in woman-to-doctor and woman-to-woman conversations that one's period can get less, and it can also become more? The experience is individualized and varies among women. Why live in the dark?

This transmission of information between the generations and generally between women is what is encouraged by the feminist movement, but discouraged by western culture; there are just some topics that you do not discuss in good company, and who would want to discuss menopause with bad company?[186] Further, since the conscious destruction of the female healer and midwife industry, untrained female-to-female transmission of medical knowledge regarding sexuality and reproduction in all it facets has been historically condemned by the medical profession. To demonstrate this point, Kaufert examines a once popular guide on menopause and Estrogen: *A Doctor Discusses Menopause and Estrogens* (1977) by M. Edward Davis, MD.[187] In this text, Davis follows the tradition of doctors who urge women against reasoning out their own menopause experience. Rather, she is encouraged to

---

[185] Guest, and Jankeys. "Abnormal-Bleeding-During-Peri-Menopause." *Everyday Health. EverydayHealth.com.* September 2002. Web. 3 March 2012.
[186] All the topics we are told not to speak about in good company, religion, politics, and body functions, are normally the exact topics that we should be discussed in all society. Silence equals the abandonment of personal power.
[187] Dr. M. E. Davis was a Professor Emeritus from the Department of Obstetrics and Gynecology, University of Chicago.

be more of a passive patient who listens to her doctor's correct and expert advice:

> According to Davis, medical expertise extends into all aspects of the life of the menopausal woman. It is as a physician that he advises her to change her make-up (p. 21), see her dentist (p. 22), watch her figure (p. 24), acquire new interests (p. 53), not interfere in the lives of her children (p. 2), and stimulate her husband's waning sexual appetite.[188]

Although the medical community's attitude toward menopause has changed since 1977, subjective experience demonstrates that this embedded attitude regarding information transmission among women on the topics of menstruation, sex, and menopause has not changed much.[189] Even today, if I wish to read and educate myself on perimenopause, I am confronted with book after book written by gynecologists, nutritionists, and drug companies because the publishing industry deems their ethos more respectable than the everyday woman's knowledge regarding these experiences.

After doctors, advertisers and drug companies are apparently the next important authority on the topic of menopause. We women are faced with commercial after commercial telling us how we can best manage this reproductive downtime of life: through drugs, makeup, weight loss solutions, cosmetic surgery, and even shakes. In 2009, a *Jack in the Box* commercial informed menopausal women that they could avoid becoming "street rat crazy" by drinking one

---

[188] Kaufert, p. 155.

[189] Agee, Eve. "Menopause and the Transmission of Women's Knowledge: African American and White Women's Perspectives." *Medical Anthropology Quarterly, New Series.* 14:1 (March, 2000). Pp 73-95. Print.

of their frozen drinks.[190] Next, as one Estroven Commercial suggests: "the all natural ingredients in Estroven are clinically shown to help you spend less time on your symptoms and more on your journey."[191] For advertisers and drug companies, reproductive aging and "feeling old" are one in the same, and a feeling of youth will only return with the use of this or that product.

The commercials tell us that we are old, us menopausal women, but that fountain of youth remedies might exist. In these commercials, not only are women old in actuality, but also spiritually. A tired jammer wanting to call off the jam one minute before time is up. This is the cultural presentation of aging women. Researching this topic, I was rather surprised to learn that contrary to the many advertisements presenting the menopausal woman as feeling "old" before her discovery of their magical product, most menopausal women do not feel old simply because they are menopausal. Verily, like the connection made by many commercials, I too had somehow assumed a connection. Heather E. Dillaway, Department Chair of the College of Liberal Arts and Science at Wayne State University, in her article, "Menopause is the 'Good Old': Women's Thoughts About Reproductive Aging," found that "aging and menopause seemed like distinct and separate processes to women . . . thus most did not feel old upon reproductive aging."[192] Hm? I can tell you, Mom felt old. In fact, she felt old, useless, and discarded by society. But did her menopause amplify this fact for her? Upon reflection, no it did not. When I consider the point in time when Mom really started to feel old, I must concede that this fear of being the

---

[190] "Jack In the Box Menopause Commercial." Posted by Eikriderforever. 28 April 2009. YouTube. Web. 28 March 2012.
[191] "Menopausel and / Estroven Commercial." Uploaded by *virginia316*. 22 April 2008. YouTube. Web. 28 March 2012.
[192] Dillaway, Heather E. "Menopause is the 'Good Way': Women's Thoughts About Reproductive Aging." *Gender & Society*. 19:3 (2005), pp. 398-417. p. 405.

crone (without the positive definition of the crone as wise woman, we've done away with that kindness as well) started in her early 40s, as it did with myself, before menopause. So what made her feel old ... made me feel old? ... Advertising and the cultural dialogue around women and aging. As Carol Cohn once observed while living and working around defense intellectuals, finding her thought processes changing because of it, "as I learned their language, as I became more and more engaged with their information and their arguments, I found that my own thinking was changing."[193] Yes! Advertising made one feel old, not reproductive aging. Menopause was then a separate and different insult. After all, how can you not hate your body for seemingly failing you? Now that I am maturing, I am experiencing many of the same "I'm feeling old" issues my mom felt, and it is because of the values embedded in our cultural discourse regarding aging – values that center upon a youth worshiping culture, a culture more likely to spend money spontaneously. There is, after all, a reason we often associate wisdom with age. But wisdom offers the aging woman little when she is consumed with the rhetoric of aging.

It is difficult to age in our society because we are a youth oriented, obsessed culture. This message and cultural information is especially pronounced in commercials and ads. When I was younger, I was targeted for everything: food, smokes, alcohol, clothing, music, dance clubs, credit cards and restaurants ... sexy bras and lingerie. Now that I am older, commercials aimed toward my age include makeup commercials on how to hide signs of aging, creams that erase wrinkles (yeah right, like that can really happen Mr. Medicine Man), hair dying commercials to do away with the gray, weight loss commercials, mood commercials, plastic surgery to zap

---

[193] Cohn, Carol. "Sex and Death in the Rational World of Defense Intellectuals." *Gender and Scientific Authority*. Barbara Laslett, Sally G. Kohlstedt, Helen Longio, and Evelynn Hammonds Eds. Chicago: University of Chicago Press: p. 183. Print.

varicose veins, and revival by face lift commercials: "Be a cougar, get a face lift today!" I also have to deal with adult incontinence or "I've gotta go" commercials. Finally, there are the retirement planning and RV commercials; I don't mind these as much. Collectively, except for the RV sales pitch, I am given one message: you are old and you got to find a way to be young again, or you are screwed, baby! As mentioned above, around the time my mom hit forty, she used to get pissed off at the television set. She would stomp into the living room and tell everyone watching to either "turn that TV off, or mute the goddamn commercials!" I never understood her hostility toward television commercials until I got older. I mean, we can all tune the commercials out, right? Wrong. In any case, she never spoke about it, but I suspect she resented the commercials targeting her age. It was also around forty that she started to ask me if she needed a face-lift. I would always say no, suggesting how silly it was to even think of such a thing: "Mom, only insecure people get face lifts! Age gracefully for goodness sake." But now that I am well into my forties, I am muting the commercials, demanding that the TV be shut off, and I am looking at my eyes for a "lift." I am also checking my pubic hair to make sure it is still there. "God can you hear me? It's me, Rebecca. Can you please reinforce my pubes?" Why on earth do I allow these damn commercials to have such a sway over me?

One of my favorite books is by environmentalist Bill McKibben: *The Age of Missing Information.*[194] This book is about an experiment that McKibben conducted, contrasting the experience of watching twenty-four hours of television compared to spending a single day out in nature. In his book, McKibben's offers a profound observational truth: "But TV is cumulative, and over a lifetime ten minutes here and there of watching fishing or car racing or *Divorce Court* has added up to

---

[194] McKibben, Bill. *The Age of Missing Information.* New York: Random House trade paperback, 2006. Print.

a lot of hours and had a certain effect on us all."[195] Now what if we were to exchange "fishing," "car racing," and *Divorce Court* with sagging skin commercials, incontinence commercials, and plastic surgery commercials? There is most certainly a cumulative effect that these commercials have on our psyche, and this effect takes place the very first time we sit in front of a TV set; it invades our life until the day we die:

"Turn the goddamn thing off, will you pleazeeeee!"

It is not only the TV, but all the ads we are bombarded with have a cumulative effect on our attitudes about aging. Ads on billboards, on the radio, on your sister's tee shirt, in magazines, TV guide, on Twitter, Facebook, and all over the Internet influences us continuously. Yes, even advertisements in the air with airplanes, on the side of cars and vans, at your favorite sports arena, and in your children's schools. All of these different forms of advertising affect us, reinforcing certain ideals and values in mass culture. As McKibben writes regarding TV, I could simply write the same regarding mass advertisements:

> [Advertisements are] a pipeline to the modern world, and a convenient shorthand for some of its features. Still, that does not mean that [advertisements] merely reflect our society. By virtue of [their] omnipresence, it also constantly reinforces certain ideas. It is less an art form than the outlet for a utility--like the faucet on a sink that connects you to the river.[196]

Even when I think I am ignoring commercials, they are speaking to me about my now gray hair, the lines on my skin, and the age spots on my hands. They speak to the younger generation as well. One Twitter user, @RayMaserati, proclaimed regarding Beyonce's pregnancy: "Beyonce is

---

[195] Ibid, p. 14.
[196] Ibid, p. 17.

189

pregnant? It's about time. She about to go into menopause."[197] The Beyonce pregnancy topic was trending on Twitter and everyone seemed amazed, many delighted as well, that this 30 year old (that's right, she was born in 1981 so she must be menopausal, which means I must be dead or just about) was pregnant.[198] The point is this, @RayMaserati demonstrates an attitude that is nurtured in all of us by our culture: what it means to be or get old, and this attitude is not only nurtured here in the United States! As McKibben observes,

> ... even in the poorest countries advertising is constant. According to a recent article in the magazine *Adbusters*, in the Ivory Coast, 'advertising is helping to change the Ivorian attitude toward aging, making women fear looking older and undermining the traditional respect for elders' -- which of course represents a significant loss of information because the old people are the wise people, the people who understand the land.[199]

Genderism and ageism is a global problem.

The Gender Ads Project is an interesting website designed by cultural anthropologist Dr. Scott A. Lukas.[200] This site presents an opportunity to learn how to read and interpret the ads we are bombarded with daily. Focusing on Katherine Toland Frith's text *Undressing the Ad: Reading Culture in*

---

[197] Ray Maserati (@RayMaserati). "Beyonce is pregnant? It's about time. She about to go into menopause." 17 August 2011. Tweet.
[198] Wete, Brad. "Beyonce's Pregnancy Reveal Breaks Twitter Record: Why Do We Care So Much?" *Entertainment Weekly*. 30 August 2011. Web. 30 August 2011.
[199] McKibben, p. 50.
[200] Lukas, Scott A. "Gender Ads Project." *Genderads.com*. 2011. Web. 10 September 2012.

Advertising,[201] and Erving Goffman's text on *Gender Advertisements,*[202] we are instructed to look at the message layers in advertisements, including the embedded codes/ideological frames present. Dr. Lukas asks us to analyze advertisements by examining three different types of meanings: the surface meaning, the advertiser's intended meaning, and the cultural ideological meaning. The surface meaning equals our overall impression of the advertisement, including what we see, hear, and read. The advertiser's intended message is the sales pitch, and the ideological meaning concerns society's cultural knowledge and assumptions that we, the audience, bring with us to the advertisement. This cultural knowledge helps the advertisement speak to us, each of us directly. It's this third category that I am particularly interested in, since the cultural or ideological meaning of commercials reinforce socialized information, and how we view ourselves. The mystery is solved, I am feeling old because I am told from so many sources that I am old, not because I am perimenopausal, or menopausal: commercials, life insurance companies, and even my dear, well-meaning students send me this "you are old" message: "Cindy Lauper's 'Be Bop'? That is such an oldie Dr. McCarthy." "An oldie but a goodie, just like me!" There are times when I crack an age joke at my expense so that I can break this age ice. So I can move on. But all of this aging rhetoric has made me hyper aware of my age, of getting older, of "maturing" as the PC crowd phrases it. Nevertheless, when I am allowed to ignore my age, I feel like me, with the same tastes and preferences for living life. I even feel young. Dare I? … Young enough for roller derby?

After my husband left me for work on my forty-fifth birthday, and my pets settled in for their morning nap, I

---

[201] Frith, Katherine T. *Undressing the Ad: Reading Culture in Advertising.* New York: Lang, 1997. Print.
[202] Goffman, Erving. *Gender Advertisements.* Cambridge, Mass: Harvard University Press, 1979. Print.

walked into the bathroom to do my own grooming. I looked in the mirror and traced my lips with a finger. I had a cold sore on my upper lip, and so I put Camphor and Neosporin on it: "Work your magic fast, please," I prayed. This increase of acne is apparently part of my new "condition." Indeed, it was a week before my birthday that I was "officially" diagnosed as being perimenopausal.[203] I went to my doctor because of how crazy my periods were. As my sister and I joke, Aunt Flow likes to overstay her welcome. Over the last few years, I have noticed many changes in myself that concern me: erratic and long periods, acne, "fuzzy" memory issues, weight gain, whitening hair, hair loss (not down there, yet. Thank goodness), a droopy right eye lid, having to go pee more often, and I no longer sleep through the night, waking up often four or more times. Also, I am crabby. That's right, I encompass a bad attitude about aging and the circus act around the process. It was time to do something about it all, and since I couldn't afford a face-lift, a boob job, or new tattoo, I did the next best thing: I joined a roller derby team. At forty-five I strapped on skates, pads, a crash helmet, and took to the rink, with all my speed and aggression in tow. To my surprise, other women over forty had the same idea, we even have a Facebook page: "Derby over 40." There is one remarkable thing about the community of derby playing women: they talk. They talk about everything. I started to take back what I had lost, a kind of power over self and ability. On the floor I am "The Mental Pause," a derby nickname powered by irony, since I pause for no one. This hag's a jammer, and during a bout on my forty-sixth birthday, this crone succeeded in racking up four grand slams in a row — working to reverse a mental cycle of obsoleteness.

When I was younger, I consumed all bits of Wiccan philosophy, including discussions about the cycles of a woman's life. I loved the feminist/mythological imagery of the

---

[203] *Men pausis* actually means "month to end," and *peri* means "near."

maiden, the mother, and the crone. Part of the triple goddess image that was to reflect each phase in a woman's life. The phases represent a beautiful rite of passage, where we earn our place in each moment of time, including the crone, who was often written about in these texts as the wise woman who helps her younger counterpart on the journey through life. This new age hag has held Ra's great seeing eye, and is now a fountain of knowledge to be loved, revered, cared for and respected. Hell, with this rhetoric, who would not want to be a crone? But this definition of the crone holds a rather modern feminist spin on what is traditionally a derogatory term applied to old(er) women. Consider the traditional hag image fashioned from the ancient Greek story about the evil three blind, Gray Hags who fought over a single eye for sight, but lost it to the great hero Perseus. This is the "time-honored" hag/crone as evil witch presentation. Keeping with this tradition, *The Oxford English Dictionary* states that a crone is a "cantankerous" or "mischievous" woman, a "withered old woman," an "old ewe" (as in "to pick out and reject [the old sheep] from the flock") - Ouch![204] *Wikipedia* makes the interesting and accurate observation that the crone is thought of as either helpful or difficult. She can be obsolete or magical. Wise or simply old. A saint or a bitch; a normal woman? But she is always marginalized because of her place in the reproductive cycle and her approaching death. She is the hag.[205] But why should the hag, the crone be such a withering, hateful image? Indeed, I want to redeem the hag and hand her the Eye of Ra. She shall sit next to Sophia, the great lady of wisdom. By redeeming the hag, we control our destiny, including information. As the crone, I want to transmit that

---

[204] *The Compact Edition of the Oxford English Dictionary.* Complete Text Reproduced Micrographically; Volume 1, A-O. New York: Oxford University Press. 1973, P. 607: 1185. Print.
[205] Wikipedia contributors. "Crone." *Wikipedia, The Free Encyclopedia.* 26 February 2011. Web. 30 August 2011.

information to others, breaking the silence that holds so many women hostage. It is time to jam through the blockers of image creation and medical reproductive knowledge. This hag can see no better place for redemption than on a derby track.

"Bank It"
(Sung to the WWI Tune, "Over There.")

I know I've lost my mind, lost my mind, lost my mind.
I'm skating all the time, all the time, all the time.
Mental Pause is gaining track, passin'-on through as you go
splat? Blockers in my way, in my way, in my way.
But I am fast today, yes today, yes today.
My skate bitch provides a whip; I pound on through,
giving you the slip.

Chorus
That crone can skate, that hag's first rate, she cleared the track, and that's a fact, no time to wait. The smell of sweat and hairspray; her quad skates obey, and *Mental Pause* is no lightweight. Don't be irate, yo sparring mate, it's just my fate, oh yes my fate, this diamond skate. I'm getting older, so very bolder; this crone to hag is at the threshold gate.

INDEX

About the Author

Image by Mona Concepcion, 2010.

Rebecca Lea McCarthy (1966 - Present) was born in Tucson, AZ, and has since lived all over the U.S. She holds a PhD from Florida Atlantic University's Public Intellectual Program, a Masters of Liberal Studies from Rollins College, and a BFA in Acting from Cornish College of the Arts. McFarland published her first book, *Origins of the Magdalene Laundries: An Analytical History*, 2010. Her writings cover the topics of women's issues, ethics, theatre, cosmopolitanism, and digital recall. In her off hours, McCarthy skates roller derby in Washington State.

www.ingramcontent.com/pod-product-compliance
Lightning Source LLC
Chambersburg PA
CBHW070006300526
45794CB00001B/206